Praise for
Arnold M. Patent's
You Can Have It All

"As you read this book, you will learn that you are the only one who determines the path your life takes. *YOU CAN HAVE IT ALL* is an excellent map to lead you on a joyful journey."

—James Bolen, editor of *New Realities*

"Arnold is a wonderful and inspiring writer, speaker, and human being. He walks his talk."

—Justin and Michael Toms, New Dimensions Radio

"Arnold's simple and profound techniques for opening the doors to material and spiritual abundance are some of the most effective I have ever encountered."

—Jim Morningstar, Ph.D., author of
Breathing in Light and Love

"Arnold has been doing wonderful work for years."

—Louise L. Hay, author of
You Can Heal Your Life

"After a decade of dabbling in today's metaphysical literature, I have yet to find a more powerful, simple, and succinct introduction to spiritual principles than that provided by Arnold Patent."

—John Hatch, originator of the Foundation for International
Community Assistance

ARNOLD M. PATENT

YOU CAN HAVE IT ALL

A SIMPLE GUIDE TO A JOYFUL AND ABUNDANT LIFE

John Gray, Ph.D.
Foreword

John Hatch
Introduction

POCKET BOOKS
New York   London   Toronto   Sydney   Tokyo   Singapore

POCKET BOOKS, a division of Simon & Schuster Inc.
1230 Avenue of the Americas, New York, NY 10020

Copyright © 1995 by Arnold M. Patent

Published by arrangement with Beyond Words Publishing, Inc.

All rights reserved, including the right to reproduce
this book or portions thereof in any form whatsoever.
For information address Beyond Words Publishing, Inc.,
4443 NE Airport Road, Hillsboro, OR 97124

ISBN: 0-671-00076-4

First Pocket Books trade paperback printing January 1997

10 9 8 7 6 5 4 3 2 1

POCKET and colophon are registered trademarks
of Simon & Schuster Inc.

Cover design by Brigid Pearson

Printed in the U.S.A.

This revised edition is dedicated to the many people whose commitment to Universal Principles and the Mutual Support Network demonstrates that opening our hearts is natural, feels wonderful and connects us to our true power.

TABLE OF CONTENTS

SECTION FIVE — SELF-LOVE

SECTION SIX — MEANS AND ENDS

SECTION SEVEN — THE SUPPORT GROUP

SECTION EIGHT — BEYOND BASICS

FOREWORD

I was honored when Arnold Patent asked me to write a foreword to *You Can Have It All*, because I feel a connection to Arnold and to his work. I am moved by this book because I know what Arnold says is true—I have often asked for and received support from the Universe—and feel our lives have taken similar paths.

Reading *You Can Have It All*, it became clear to me that we share a mission to dispel the confusion that can seem overwhelming in life and replace it with clarity and hope. Although we were inspired in different ways, we were both led by the pain we were feeling to a point where we could clearly see that we had a responsibility to offer help to people who are locked within their hearts and share the tools we had discovered which we can all use to free ourselves.

The Universal Principles explained in *You Can Have It All* make sense. They even seem simple as you are guided through them. It is invigorating to read this book. Like diving into cool water on a hot day, *You Can Have It All* is refreshing, renewing our awareness of the beauty and perfection of the Universe—and the role each of us plays within it. We all choose the lives we are living, and for those who genuinely wish to live lives of balance and abundance, this book will certainly be a powerful tool.

In the preface of my book *Men, Women and Relationships*, I wrote that I dedicated it to "those light bearers who are already on the outside trying to help others free themselves." Arnold Patent is a wonderful example of that kind of person. The love, compassion, and work he put into *You Can Have It All* is evidence that he has truly dedicated himself to making a difference in people's lives. This book is an act of courage, the embodiment of Arnold's commitment to helping people meet the greatest challenge each of us faces, living the fulfilled lives we are all capable of living.

John Gray

INTRODUCTION

I am deeply honored to have been asked to contribute an introduction to this latest revision of Arnold Patent's *You Can Have It All*. I do this as a true labor of love, for no single book has had a greater influence on my life. Not only have I reread it many times, but I consult it frequently. For years a volume of this remarkable book has rested on my nightstand for instant reference or inspiration. I even carry around in my briefcase a synopsis of its content, handwritten on four sheets of yellow notebook paper. Some of the Universal Principles enunciated by Arnold Patent have become virtual mantras in my daily life: (1) Everything in the Universe is energy; (2) Everything is perfect; (3) I start from completion; (4) Abundance is my natural state; (5) I am responsible for everything that happens; (6) There is no right and wrong; and (7) In forgiving I remove my energy blocks. Naturally, like so many students, I have applied these principles inconsistently; but even so, they have proven remarkably effective. These principles helped me to weather a divorce. They helped me to overcome serious indebtedness. They helped me to finally create a nurturing and loving marriage. And these principles continue to support me in my professional life, where I am fulfilling my purpose by bringing to fruition a personal vision and commitment to heal the world of severe poverty.

You Can Have It All was the first self-improvement book I ever began, much less finished. It proved to be a perfect place to start. After a decade of dabbling in today's metaphysical literature, I have yet to find a more powerful, simple and succinct introduction to spiritual principles than that provided by Arnold Patent. But now, in this latest revision of an already exceptional book, Arnold's gifts of insight and support are communicated even more effectively than before. Many chapters have been reorganized to present their central ideas even more powerfully. The author has taken his original buffet of some fifty concise chapters and regrouped them into helpful, appetizing sections. The Feeling Exercise, which Arnold introduced in his 1991 revision, now runs as a central theme integrating the entire book, providing us with a powerful new tool for accessing the power of our divine essence—our birthright of love, peace and joy.

Furthermore, behind this book additional guidance is available through the author's successful workshops and rapidly growing international network of mutual support groups. Before I met Arnold Patent for the first time, I carried in the glove compartment of my Mazda several cassettes of one of his seminars. During over 30,000 miles of driving throughout northern Arizona in the spring of 1985, when I was a regional organizer for Hands Across America, I played these tapes until I nearly knew them by heart. Eventually I got to attend a Patent workshop in Tucson in 1986, shortly after my son died. Two years later I attended another workshop in Phoenix. I would like to share an experience from the second workshop because it also influenced my life. I remember taking my nervous turn at the microphone—in front of about 300 people—to ask Arnold a question. Earlier that year I had been experiencing serious, chronic back pain, which I knew was caused by an energy block, but I didn't understand its origin. I had mostly forgiven my parents. I had overcome the anguish of my son's death. I was now very happily remarried. In my professional life I was encountering unprecedented success. My life had never felt more abundant and purposeful. So why was my back killing me?

By this time Arnold knew I had been a Peace Corps volunteer. He knew I had devoted over twenty years of my adult life to working overseas in foreign-assistance programs attempting to help low-income people. So Arnold answered my question with surgical precision, and it went something like this: "John, you do not yet see that poverty is part of the perfection of the Universe. You have been waging your personal war on poverty for many years. Your body is simply registering the accumulated discomfort of battling an illusion you have chosen to invest with your power. *I suggest you try forgiving poverty rather than making war on it.*"

Since that day I *have* learned to see poverty as perfect. And my back-pain problem has disappeared. I have come to accept the perfection of the human holocaust of 60,000 children dying each day worldwide from hunger-related disease, the victims of severe poverty. This tragedy is a perfect opportunity for teaching humanity the consequences of its belief in the illusion of our separateness. It is a perfect opportunity for the poor to support each other in overcoming the illusion that their scarcity is inescapable. Finally, it is a perfect opportunity for the rest of us to support the poor in this purpose, while learning to open our hearts to the oneness of the Universe.

Because *You Can Have It All* taught me that the Universe is a mutual support system, I have attempted to integrate the support group concept as the pillar of my work with the poor overseas. The Foundation for International Community Assistance (FINCA), a non-profit agency that I started in 1984, currently works in sixteen developing countries, where it has benefited more than 60,000 extremely poor families and is now virtually doubling its funding and coverage every year. In a nutshell, FINCA makes self-employment loans of $50-$300 to low-income mothers (mostly single heads of households) so that they can generate an extra $2 to $3 of income per day, which goes directly into improving the diet, health and living conditions of their children. The program's loan repayment rate is a remarkable 99 percent. Its borrowers are also saving at a rate of over 5 percent per month. FINCA's clients are organized in support groups of 20 to 50 members—popularly known as "village banks"—which hold their weekly meetings in the home or patio of one of their leaders. These village bankers select their own members, prepare their own bylaws, keep their own accounts and manage all the funds. In sum, the unbankable have become bankers themselves. As they witness the day-by-day growth of their business income, their savings, and the health and welfare of their children, these mothers are becoming greatly empowered. Each can now see her personal path out of poverty; she knows that it is only a matter of time before her self-sufficiency is assured. Each is learning that *she* holds the key to her own success, that *she can have it all*, and that indeed *she already has it all!*

Here in Guatemala City, my wife, Mimi, has been designing an entirely new but complementary technology for village bankers, which she calls "women's empowerment modules." Yes, these too depend a lot on Universal Principles gleaned from the writings of Arnold Patent. Most importantly, they focus on getting in touch with feelings. Through the use of role-playing, positive affirmations of mutual support and weekly homework assignments, Mimi's training modules are changing forever the negative images impoverished women have come to believe about themselves. They are teaching women how to create more positive relationships, how to communicate constructively with children and spouses, how to better protect their families from alcoholism, domestic violence, AIDS and other health risks, and how to support each other in attempting behavioral changes that can transform their lives.

I believe with all my heart that by the year 2005, some 200 million severely poor families worldwide will have gained access to village bank loans, learned how to save, and will be sufficiently empowered—economically and interpersonally—to virtually eliminate forever some of the planet's oldest scourges. A world healed of severe poverty is the gift we most wish to leave our grandchildren.*

I pray that one day the experience in self-empowerment of the poor—which we are creating overseas—can be brought back to assist people in the inner cities of the United States. Arnold Patent believes, and I wholeheartedly agree, that we will soon have many opportunities to use our respective models together. If we truly believe the principle of "starting from completion," then the fact that we can imagine such a mutually supportive partnership means that it already exists.

Thank you, Arnold Patent, for teaching us how perfect, and how limitlessly abundant, is our sandbox!

John Hatch

---

*Those motivated to support these efforts are invited to contact FINCA for more information. Write to 901 King Street, Alexandria, Virginia 22314, or telephone (703) 836-5516, or fax (703) 836-5366.

ACKNOWLEDGMENTS

The latest revision of *You Can Have It All* is a perfect example of mutual support. Kathy Hart, as editor, felt inspired to reorganize the book to create a smoother and clearer flow in the presentation of the Universal Principles. I, as author, felt inspired to write new material to reflect my expanded understanding of these principles. Our support of each other has resulted in a book that not only is more fun to read, but that offers a guide to fill your life with the ease and joy of playing together in mutual support.

Many other people have contributed their loving support over the years, and Selma and I express our deep gratitude to:

- those to whom we can reach out to help us prepare for an upcoming event;
- those who travel thousands of miles yearly to attend workshops in the United States and abroad;
- and those who shower us with countless personal kindnesses.

We hope that each person who reads this book will feel invited to join this loving circle.

SECTION ONE

THE BASICS

1

DISCOVERING PRINCIPLE

For the first fifty years of my life, I did exactly what I thought I was supposed to do. In practicing law, which I did for more than twenty-five years, I struggled to deal with my clients' problems and with real estate investments. It is true that I earned enough money to live a model life in an affluent suburb of New York City, but what a price I paid!

The model life, instead of bringing me joy, brought only pain, which I carried with me all the time. Clinically, doctors could find nothing wrong with me. Yet so great was my discomfort that I began to search for a way to make myself well.

I started by taking vitamins and changing my diet, but that didn't seem to help. With my focus on diet and vitamins, I came across a very sophisticated nutritional program that intrigued me, and I flew to Chicago to learn more about it. During four days of intensive study, I decided to go on the program. I took at least a hundred pills a day, including vitamins, supplements, digestive enzymes, glandular stimulants, and so forth. After a while, I noticed that I felt better, so I stayed on the program for a year and a half.

The most significant part of the program, though I didn't realize it at the time, was a daily regimen of meditation, based on the belief that stress is the single most destructive factor in one's life and that meditation is the single most effective and beneficial way to deal with stress. I started meditating and continued for the full year and a half that I remained on the program.

During this time, I began to learn what were for me new ideas. Known for many, many years, these were the basic laws that explain how the Universe works. These "Universal Principles," as I now call them, are simple, straightforward and easy to understand. However, since they are contrary to most of the teachings of our society, they are generally ignored.

Having learned how to accept challenges as a lawyer, investor and businessman, I was now ready to undertake what seemed like my greatest challenge—adopting Universal Principles as my day-to-day guidelines for life. And so began the second chapter of my life.

I applied the same perseverance to the practice of these principles that I had applied to the nutritional program and noticed even further improvement in the way I felt. By this time, the discomfort in my body was greatly reduced, yet I realized that I was far from rid of it. I began to appreciate how much pain I had experienced all those years. No wonder I had so often been uptight, jumpy, impatient and unhappy.

As I got further into the practice of Universal Principles, I discontinued the nutritional program. Not only did I sustain the improvement I had achieved, but I continued to improve. The improvement has continued, with every indication that it will do so until every last bit of discomfort has been released from my body.

I began to share these ideas with others who were interested. I soon realized that my way of stating and explaining the principles was very clear and convincing, owing, in part, to my legal training and experience. After all, I had been trained to apply a body of legal principles to a variety of personal and business situations. I had simply replaced the body of principles.

After being encouraged to continue to present these ideas, I offered a correspondence course to people in different parts of the country. In the process of expanding the course, a friend who was supportive of me suggested that I offer a workshop to teach these concepts. Following my first workshop, I realized that I had found my ideal vehicle and outlet for presenting Universal Principles.

I started with evening workshops that lasted about two and a half hours. Later I adopted a full weekend format, beginning Friday evening and ending late Sunday afternoon.

These weekends have been so successful in demonstrating the power of mutual support that I am organizing this book as I do a workshop to give you the opportunity of having a similar experience.

The Weekend Begins

Selection of the site is important. I favor a room that is light and airy, with space to conduct part of the program outdoors in mild weather. After registration, often with live music in the background, the workshop begins.

The ages and backgrounds of the participants vary greatly, from six-month-old infants to ninety-year-old youngsters, with collars of all colors from white to blue and all those in between. College professors, artists, businesspeople, musicians, doctors, lawyers, actors and homemakers attend the workshops. It is exciting to watch this broad cross-section of people quickly and easily become a family for the weekend, freely offering support of all kinds to one another.

I start the formal part of the evening with a presentation of a number of the Universal Principles. Next, participants introduce themselves to people sitting near them. Later in the evening, they join in small (four to six people) support groups. These groups meet several times during the weekend and offer participants the opportunity to practice the principles set forth at the seminar.

Saturday morning we are ready for the first of many question-and-answer periods, which help participants learn how to apply these principles to their personal lives.

Since I do not use notes, I rely on the needs, desires and energies of the participants to direct me in the presentation of the material. Although the basic material covered is always the same, each workshop is unique in the ways that it varies from its predecessors.

While the material is ostensibly presented from mind to mind, I like to ease its reception by offering live music and movement during the weekend. I suggest you take a similar approach. Please read small amounts between breaks. Listen to music, take a walk, stretch or do exercises periodically. To encourage you, I'll offer reminders.

Now we are ready for your private workshop to begin. Settle in your chair, take a deep breath, and realize that all of this material is natural to us. It is as natural as a child playing a game.

2

THE REAL
GAME OF LIFE

Life has often been compared to a game, and this analogy is useful. And what is the purpose of any game? To have fun. But in order to have fun playing a game, we first have to learn the rules and then, through practice, master them.

There are a number of games being played simultaneously in our society. The most popular one is the competitive-adversarial game. We have all learned the rules of that game, and many people have done very well at mastering them.

But as more and more people are discovering, the competitive-adversarial game isn't fun. And many are choosing not to play it. In response to those who have chosen to drop out of the game, there have been attempts made to change some of the rules. The reason these attempts haven't worked too well is that the new rules don't fit the old game.

The solution is simpler than we realize, because not only is there a game that is fun to play, but it is one that is natural to us. This is the game of mutual support—the real game of life.

In this book I describe the real game, and I explain the rules. Once you agree that this *is* the real game, and you are willing to learn the rules and play the game, the level of mastery you achieve will depend upon your level of intention.

In my experience over the past fifteen years, as soon as you make the commitment to yourself to play the real game, the Universe will acknowledge that commitment and offer such generous support that the quality of your life will improve substantially and will continue to improve with each step you take.

There is no limit to the amount you can improve the quality of your life. No matter how wonderful it might seem at any level you achieve, the possibility for further improvement always exists, because the game never ends.

When you choose to play the real game, you allow yourself the pleasure and enjoyment that comes from playing the one game that offers fulfillment to each and every player. In the game of mutual support, everybody wins.

※　※　※

To master the real game, we begin by becoming familiar with the playing field on which the game is played. Thus, I'll start by describing the Universe, this magnificent entity that is our home and of which we are all a part.

3

───────■───────

THE UNIVERSE

O ur Universe includes everything in existence from the largest galaxy to the tiniest particle. Each "thing"—seen as well as unseen—is composed of energy. Another way to say this is that the Universe is a limitless expression of energy.

Within all energy, and thus within everything in the Universe, is a loving Intelligence that is infinite, eternal and purposeful. This Infinite Intelligence, or God, or simply love—there are many names for the essence of energy—is the motivating force, the source of all creative expression in the Universe.

Paradoxical as it may seem, human beings, as expressions of this loving essence, have the free will to create circumstances that appear to be anything but loving. The choice to create pain and chaos does not mean that we are malicious or stupid, just wildly creative and temporarily forgetful of who we really are.

However, even these excursions into chaos and pain are purposeful. For the Universe, in Its infinite wisdom, assures that we remain in the consciousness of whatever we create until the reflection of that circumstance drives us to look inside ourselves—where we discover the loving, eternal essence that we truly are.

Even when we are unaware of our essence, we are not separate from it. And we are never separate from each other, for we are all connected, essence to essence, all the time. This is the true meaning of the word Oneness. Stated in colloquial terms, Oneness means that we are all in this game of life together, and we are all on the same side.

Furthermore, through our connectedness, we influence each other all of the time, and the way we influence each other follows clearly defined laws. When understood, these laws, which I call Universal Principles, demonstrate that we are all part of a mutual support system.

Universal Principles are the perfect guidelines for life within this remarkable system. Following these principles places each of us in conscious alignment with our Universe and with everything and everyone in It.

Let's look now at these Universal Principles in greater detail, starting with the concept of energy.

4

ENERGY

The basic component of the Universe, energy, occurs in either materialized or unmaterialized form. The things that we see around us, such as cars, houses, books and trees, are examples of materialized energy. All energy that is not in materialized form makes up the balance of the energy in the Universe.

Both states of energy are more similar in form than appears to the naked eye. Even those objects that seem most solid, such as steel beams and concrete walls, appear as molecules in motion when viewed under high-powered microscopes.

All energy vibrates. The lower the vibration, the more density there is within the form. The higher the vibration, the more expansive the energy within the form.

What else do we know about energy? Since everything in the Universe is energy, we are always interacting with it.

Generally speaking, there are two ways to interact with energy. We can either align with the energy flowing around and through us, or we can resist the flow of that energy.

We resist the flow of energy when we choose to interpret life in ways that lead us to struggle not only with the natural abundance all around us but with each other. Resisting the flow of energy lowers our vibration and causes us discomfort.

On the other hand, when we choose to align with the free flow of energy, we feel at peace. In this state of free-flowing energy and peacefulness, we are open to the Infinite Intelligence of the Universe, which is contained in all energy. Because we are all composed of energy, this Intelligence is always available to us.

Accepting the fact that this Intelligence is always available to us encourages us to open ourselves to It. We feel and hear this Intelligence when our minds are quiet and we are in a state of inner calmness.

It is also in this state of inner calmness that we allow ourselves to feel our essence—the love that we truly are. Love is synonymous with energy. Our willingness to feel love, for ourselves and others, opens us not only to the Infinite Intelligence but also to the unlimited abundance of the Universe.

Let me suggest a scene to remind you of the infinite supply of energy—love—that is always available to you to support the quality of life that you desire. See yourself in a sandbox at an ocean beach. Your sandbox is filled with sand, and there are miles of sandy beach in three directions. You give out pails of sand from your sandbox to passersby. As your supply is depleted, you reach out and refill the box with the unlimited supply of sand that is all around you.

Our Universe is always ready to provide for us whenever we reach out to It. We need only understand the principles by which It operates, and then live by these principles.

As we choose to live by Universal Principles, we experience the ease and grace of energy flowing freely around and through us. Conversely, when we select guidelines that are at variance with Universal Principles, we experience the struggle and effort of resisting the natural flow of life.

While the choice is always ours, it is helpful to know that our Infinite Intelligence is always there to encourage us to choose the natural order.

5

INFINITE INTELLIGENCE

Infinite Intelligence, which we sometimes refer to as God, is the essence in everything. Even apparently inanimate objects, such as rocks, have an essential Intelligence.

This Intelligence is responsible for creating and sustaining everything in existence. It does so lovingly, peacefully, joyfully.

The Intelligence in human beings has two aspects—awareness and feelings. When we open to our feelings and allow them to flow freely, we also allow Infinite Intelligence to flow into our awareness.

We are by nature feeling beings. We are not, as most of us were taught to believe, thinking beings.

When we choose to activate our thinking minds, we simultaneously block or limit the free flow of our feelings and thus bypass our access to Infinite Intelligence. In a society that encourages a very active thinking mind, we have learned to suppress many of our feelings and to disregard our natural access to Infinite Intelligence.

Before we become annoyed or angry at those who taught us to live our lives based on an active thinking mind, or at ourselves for accepting the instruction, we can step back and take a broader view. From this greater perspective, we can appreciate that having a conscious mind coupled with the freedom to use it in any way we wish has given us the opportunity to explore the unlimited capacity of our conscious minds. This includes the freedom to choose to create all kinds of chaos and crises. Exploration into all of the many ways we can frighten ourselves is one of the ways we, as humans, have exercised our freedom of choice.

Every choice has a consequence. By taking note of the consequences, we can choose differently. When our exploration into fear has tired us sufficiently, we are ready to begin the journey back to love, peacefulness and joy, our direct connection to Infinite Intelligence.

❧   ❧   ❧

If there is one concept that is central to the mastery of the other principles and to understanding how the Universe functions, it is the concept of perfection. In order to use this principle successfully, we must be willing to relinquish the belief that perfection is either fanciful or unrealistic.

6

———

PERFECTION

Perfection describes the way in which the Universe functions. It is a marvelous principle that allows us to see all aspects of our lives from the highest vantage point.

What are some of the indications that the Universe functions perfectly? The sun radiates just the right amount of heat and light, and we are supplied with the perfect balance of gases in the atmosphere, to support life on Earth. Our planet rotates on its axis with total precision, and without any wear and tear on itself.

Each of us has the ability to perform functions beyond human understanding, naturally and effortlessly: We secrete chemicals to digest food; we make instant complex calculations necessary to chase and catch a fly ball; we combine two cells to create another human being. We do all of these things and many more without our thinking minds having any control of the processes.

But our thinking minds do often intervene. This intervention is in the form of beliefs, which distort our perception and lead us to see in accordance with our beliefs. Still, our eyes are capable of seeing each other's perfection regardless of the outer presentation. We always have the choice to connect essence to essence, which is the true state of our being.

How can you practice the principle of perfection in your daily life, moment by moment? By going behind the outer expression and seeing yourself and everyone else as perfect just the way you are. When you practice the principle of perfection, which is the highest truth, you raise your vibrational level and allow yourself to feel your Oneness with all.

Let's take an example of a friend who has just been fired from his job and who stops by your house on his way home. He appears upset, angry and fearful. You can accept his behavior as real and play into his beliefs of powerlessness. Or you can realize that his behavior is an expression of his beliefs at this moment and that behind these beliefs is a perfect human being who is capable of experiencing the perfection of himself and his situation at any moment he chooses.

You can listen to him and accept his feelings without supporting his beliefs in his powerlessness. As you continue to see him as perfect, you allow him the opportunity to move beyond those beliefs. The outcome will depend, in part, on your willingness to focus on his perfection.

An important point about the principle of perfection is that it is available only to those who use it. Ignorance of the concept or an unwillingness to accept the truth of it deprives one of the benefits of perfection. Conversely, those who accept the principle reap the rewards of a Universe that does indeed function perfectly at all times.

PERFECTION

Whatever we believe determines the results we achieve; how we view events and people determines how we experience them. If we want to create a higher-quality life experience, one of the most effective ways to do this is to adopt the principle of perfection. Since we each require some standard to guide us in the conduct of our lives and in the decisions we make, why not choose the one that gives us the most beneficial results? The higher the standard we choose, the closer we come to total alignment with the Universe.

Accepting the perfection of the Universe encourages us to trust our Universe and everything and everyone in It, beginning with ourselves. The result is a free flow of energy around and through us, and a feeling of aliveness, which is our direct experience of perfection.

7

FREE WILL

A most significant aspect of the principle of perfection is free will or free choice. We each have the freedom to choose in each moment.

However, most of us were trained to believe that others—initially our parents and then teachers, employers and other authority figures—were more capable of making choices than we were. As we allowed others to choose for us, we gradually withdrew our trust in ourselves to make choices.

What we have lost sight of is the fact that no one can really choose for another. When we accept the choice another makes for us, that acceptance is our choice.

In truth, we always have been, and we remain, at choice in every moment. Our awareness of this truth leads us to appreciate the power in choice, a power that is always available to us.

The vehicle through which we express our free choice or free will is the conscious mind. It remains, paradoxically, the greatest tool and the greatest source of mischief in existence.

When we feel our Oneness, we allow the conscious mind to be a tool for awareness. But when we forget that we are One, our belief in separation brings up fear. And the way most people have chosen to deal with fear is to depend on our intellects to make decisions and guide our lives.

Many are now questioning that choice, and a growing number are beginning to notice the advantages of using our free will to let Infinite Intelligence guide us. Such a choice allows our lives to unfold in effortless and magnificent ways, giving the inner creativity that each of us has the chance to flower into full and free expression as an integral part of our perfect Universe.

In the process of choosing to let Infinite Intelligence lead the way, our thinking minds keep trying to entice us to re-create with our intellects a Universe that has already been created perfectly. The simplest way to quiet our intellects and connect with the beauty of our essence, our natural perfection, is to see and feel that beauty reflected back to us by others who have made the same choice.

When we consciously choose to join with others who accept that our essence is real, we quickly learn the power of mutual support to bring our essence into the forefront of our lives. Our choice also brings us into alignment with the perfect system by which the Universe operates—the system of mutual support.

8

MUTUAL SUPPORT

O ur Universe functions as a mutual support system in which each and every thing in existence relates to and affects every other thing. The planets exert gravitational forces on one another. The sun affects the growth of plants, which in turn provide food for animals. Our use of resources on our planet has an effect on the quality of the air we breathe and the water we drink. Every thought and feeling each of us has vibrates through the Universe, and that vibration has an impact on everything. We are all part of a mutual support system.

Our ability to function successfully within such a system is directly related to our willingness to recognize and accept that mutual support is indeed the nature of life. The more willing we are to accept this truth, the more fulfilling, and the more fun, life becomes for us.

Very few of us were taught that the Universe is a mutual support system. Instead, we were taught that we are naturally competitive and adversarial. We were encouraged to strike out on our own and work hard to achieve personal objectives and goals. We were given the impression that we can achieve happiness at the expense of others, or at least without caring about others. This training has led many of us to doubt, at least at times, that we can trust that our essence—love—is who we really are.

In the face of this training and the many years of living in a society that not only accepts but promotes the virtues of the competitive-adversarial system, we need a great deal of support to help us make the transition, step by step, back to what is truly natural to us—the desire to live in mutual support.

This book is designed to provide a basis of that support by explaining not only the principles that underlie mutual support, but also the ways to use these principles moment by moment to expand our trust in the loving and perfect essence that we are.

One of the first steps we can take is to remind ourselves that we always have the choice to create environments that are harmonious, nurturing and mutually supportive. This is true whether the environment is a home, a place of business, a school, a supermarket or a crowded bus. We can begin to practice the principles of mutual support anytime, anywhere. However, given the heavy emphasis in our society on competition, it may be helpful to join with others who share a commitment to living in mutual support.

There is now in existence a network of no-cost mutual support groups that meet weekly in towns and cities throughout the United States and Canada, as well as in western Europe and Australia. The great value of these groups is that they give participants a direct experience of living in mutual support. I'll talk more about the mutual support group later in the book.

For now, let's take a break.

SECTION TWO

FEELINGS

9

BELIEFS AND ILLUSIONS

The world as we currently experience it is a result of a general agreement that things really are the way we think they are. In other words, our beliefs determine our experiences.

Not so long ago, many people believed that the earth was flat and that the sun rotated around the earth. Today, a large segment of the population believes that inflation is inevitable, calories affect weight, jails curb crime, politicians are untrustworthy, and armaments create safety. The beliefs we hold today are no more real than the beliefs of five centuries ago. All beliefs are illusions.

An illusion is something that we think is real but is not. Illusions, like beliefs, can and do change from time to time. What is real, what is true, is always present.

Our essence is always present. Beneath the overlays of doubts and fears resides our real self, which is pure love. Any time we look for it in ourselves or others, we find the essence that we truly are.

Focusing our awareness on what is real is the most efficient way to move beyond our illusory beliefs. Illusions exist only because people focus energy on them. Inflation wracks an economy because people vest power in the belief that inflation is a fact of life.

All illusions rely on our vesting power in our beliefs. Our beliefs can be on the conscious or unconscious level. Beliefs that we are not even consciously aware of holding are responsible for creating many of the illusions that we experience as reality.

Whether there is common agreement or not, it is possible for anyone at any time to see beyond an illusion. This happens when the illusion is recognized for what it really is.

Take taxes as an example. Many people view taxes as a burden, as something to be avoided whenever possible. The general perception is that the lawmakers who levy taxes and the agencies of government that collect them are our opponents.

What we seem to overlook are the facts that we freely elect these lawmakers; that they are, like the rest of us, doing the best they can; and that much of our tax money goes for roads, schools, hospitals and other health and social services that help support the way of life we have chosen to live.

When we move beyond our perception of taxes as a burden, and when we connect with the essence of our lawmakers and government officials and feel our Oneness, the energy that we vested in our beliefs about taxes—energy that seemed to be outside ourselves—returns to us. Thus, we can reclaim the power we have given to the IRS whenever we are ready to do so.

ക്ക   ക്ക   ക്ക

At various times during a workshop, I invite participants to ask questions. I have included some of the questions participants frequently ask.

Question: What can I expect when I move beyond certain illusory beliefs while the people around me continue holding those beliefs?

Answer: This question points up two aspects of our lives. We function as individuals, experiencing life consistent with our personal beliefs, and we also function as part of a society that contains many groups, each of which holds beliefs. When the individual and the group differ in their beliefs, the result is interesting.

To answer the question most simply, it is possible for an individual to experience peacefulness in the midst of chaos. The more chaotic the group experience, the more deeply must the individual have mastered peacefulness.

Although each individual can achieve peacefulness on his own, the impact from the world around us is always felt. For we are all connected at the deepest levels of our beings, and we are sensitive to the energy vibrations of everyone.

Whenever the quality of someone's life improves, his energy vibrates at a higher level and each of us picks this up, even though we may not be consciously aware of the shift. Of course, the opposite is also true. Whenever anyone experiences more pain, each of us picks up this lower vibration. The composite of all of our vibrations determines the overall quality of life on the planet.

Let's look at this idea on a more personal level. Say you are annoyed at a friend for breaking a date at the last minute. At a support group meeting, you ask for support in consciousness to feel forgiveness for your friend. Through the loving support of the group, you are able to feel that forgiveness. Not only are you vibrating at a higher level, but so is the friend you were formerly annoyed at and so are the participants in the support group who have volunteered to be part of the experience.

As your life becomes more peaceful, your vibrational level increases, and the higher vibrational energy signals that you emit are picked up as comforting and supportive by those whose energy fields are denser. This serves to encourage these people to reach for higher vibrational levels within themselves, even though they may not be aware that they are doing so.

We are all seeing and feeling the demonstration of this process in myriad ways around the world. Examples include the sudden and unexplainable toppling of the Berlin Wall, the transformation of many of the communist societies, and the beginning of harmony in the Middle East. These events are a direct outgrowth of the steady increase in the number of people on the planet who are yearning for peace, as witnessed by the growing numbers of those who meditate together for peace each December 31st.

So our role is always dual—to expand beyond our own belief systems and to support others in expanding beyond theirs. In this way, we raise the level of consciousness of everyone and everything on the planet, which plays itself out as an improved quality of life for all.

❧   ❧   ❧

Since the beliefs we hold have such a strong influence on our lives, it is helpful to understand how we came to hold these beliefs.

10

———————

THE SOURCE OF BELIEFS

Most of our beliefs are handed down from generation to generation. Many of them are part of our unconscious makeup when we're born. Other beliefs we take on as we grow up, starting at an early age.

The process of taking on a belief works something like this: An event occurs for a child that generates a feeling response. The feeling is aroused by the nature of the event. If the occurrence is pleasant, such as a warm and loving hug, the child interprets the event in what we call a positive way and begins the development of one belief—the connection of an interpretation of an event with the feeling the event aroused.

If the occurrence is a reprimand for something the child is doing, such as licking an ice cream cone while some of the ice cream drips onto his shirt, the child is likely to interpret the occurrence in a negative way, and the development of another belief begins.

The difference between a random thought and a belief is the difference between any random event and an event or experience that has meaning to us at a deep level of feeling. The degree of importance each of our beliefs has for us is measured by the amount of feeling behind the belief. The feeling behind the belief is what gives the belief its power.

Our beliefs, then, are really deep feeling experiences that have a direct impact on the way we perceive the world. They also affect the quality of our lives. Since there is no limit to what we can feel, there is no limit to how joyful and abundant our lives can be.

Most of us have been taught, or have interpreted our experiences in such a way as to believe, that life is not inherently joyful and naturally abundant. As a result, we attract experiences that are consistent with such a belief. Because we tend to avoid being aware of most of our beliefs, attracting experiences that are consistent with these beliefs helps us to learn what these beliefs are.

Beliefs that misperceive the truth do not change the truth. The belief that the earth was flat was a misperception. It did not make the earth flat, but it did limit many people's mobility.

The Universe, created and kept in operation by Infinite Intelligence, continuously sends us signals to remind us of the truth of who we are and what life is really all about. These signals provide us with an incredible opportunity, for as we develop an awareness of them, we move beyond our illusory and limiting beliefs and enjoy the truth of our perfect and abundant Universe.

What are these signals? Basically, there are only two. When we are functioning in alignment with the truth, we experience a sense of comfort in our bodies. When we are out of alignment, we experience discomfort. Another way of describing the signals is to say that when we are in harmony with the Universe, we are in our hearts, and when we are out of harmony, we are in our heads.

The truth lives in our hearts. We will never know the truth by listening to our rational minds. How do we hear what our hearts have to say? Through a mechanism that each of us has—our intuition.

11

——————

INTUITION

An old friend, Phil Laut,* came up with the best definition of intuition I've heard. He said intuition is Infinite Intelligence talking to us between our thoughts. In order to receive this communication, we have to tune out the other mechanism—our thinking mind. The easiest way to do this is to focus our awareness on our feelings.

As infants, we function mostly on an intuitive basis. Since our rational society discourages the use of this mechanism, as we advance in age, we are encouraged to disregard our intuition and to rely instead on our thinking minds. We are also encouraged to close our hearts and ignore our feelings.

Mastery of the intuitive process, as with mastery of any skill, requires a clear and strong intention. To develop that intention, we begin by questioning the belief that rational thinking is superior to intuitive feel-

————

*Author of *Money Is My Friend* (Trinity Publications, 1979)

ing. We gradually shift our focus from our thoughts to our feelings. We start to notice what our intuition feels like and what it sounds like. We try following our intuition's guidance, and we take note of the results. With practice, we learn to distinguish between intuition and something that seems like it, but is really our rational mind talking.

Sometimes we have an investment in a particular result and therefore choose not to listen to or follow our intuition. For example, imagine a third-year student at a university majoring in science. One day the student discovers that what she really loves to do is create graphic designs. In order to pick up the intuitive signals that will guide her in her choice of a career, she would have to let go of her perceived need to complete her course of study as a science major.

The student's intuition may still guide her to complete her degree in science. However, she will want to be vigilantly aware of whether her choice is being influenced by her vested interest in the three years she has already devoted to obtaining a science degree.

A most significant point here is that in order to improve the quality of your life, it is important to be totally honest with yourself at all times. In a society where dishonesty is a way of life, this can be a very challenging assignment.

Exploring Intuition

A useful and pleasurable way to experience your intuition is through artistic expression. Using colored crayons, paint, chalk or pencils, allow yourself to express without any rational-mind control. Choose your colors and designs intuitively. This is a fascinating experience that will tell you a lot about yourself.

By doing a series of these artistic renderings over a period of time, you will notice a continuity in your pictures. You will begin to trust yourself to express freely. And you will connect with your intuition.

Similar creative expression can be explored through music, dance, sports or martial arts. Giving yourself opportunities to respond intuitively will help you learn what letting go feels like—another aspect of intuition. It will also teach you about trusting in the inherent perfection of the Universe.

You can support yourself in practicing Universal Principles by choosing times when you feel safe and relaxed. Becoming comfortable with the principles while painting, dancing or playing tennis is no less valuable than in any other context. Pick the times and places that are most conducive to integrating the principles. Know that the Universe supports you in keeping it simple and allowing it to be fun. Avoid waiting for crises to practice using the principles. Practice them when your life is peaceful, quiet and comfortable.

Question: You say that our vested interests make it difficult for us to follow our intuition. Can you say more about vested interests?

Answer: The commitment to vested interests is all-pervasive in our society. Careful attention is required to notice the many ways that our vested interests influence our decisions.

One of the most notable examples of vested interests occurs in the workplace. Almost everyone—professional, clerk, salesperson, executive, laborer—holds a strong belief, usually on a subconscious level, that his way of making a living has to continue in order for him to survive. So the person's thinking tends to support this belief.

As a lawyer, I remember when the idea of no-fault insurance was introduced. Because my practice did not include automobile negligence, I thought at first the proposed legislation would not affect me. It didn't take more than a few moments of additional thinking for me to ask myself the question, "What will those lawyers who can no longer support themselves with automobile negligence cases do?" I realized that many of them would branch out into real estate, my specialty.

Although I was aware of the threat that no-fault legislation posed to my livelihood, I also saw the benefits of the legislation. So I was prepared to support it. I noticed, however, that some members of my profession started publishing articles explaining all the ways the new legislation was inadequate. I sensed that their arguments were not so much offers of public support as justifications for preserving the status quo. Their underlying intention was to discredit this new legislation because it was perceived by the lawyers as a threat to their vested interests.

The concept of vested interests is significant for you as a reader of this book. You may have vested interests that are totally at variance with many of the principles described on these pages. Therefore, you will want to pay close attention to the subtle ways in which you resist accepting the value of these concepts because of your vested interests.

Remember that it is our hearts and not our heads that know the truth of Universal Principles. We hear this truth through the mechanism of our intuition. And it is through our feelings that we connect to our intuition.

❧   ❧   ❧

For many of us, emotions and feelings are a murky area that elicits confusion and often a lot of fear. However, once we understand the function of feelings and learn to tap into them, we make the profound discovery that our feelings are the source of our power, our creativity and our unlimited abundance.

12

───■───

EMOTIONS, THOUGHTS
AND FEELINGS

The subject of emotions, thoughts and feelings is an intriguing one. Understanding it broadens our understanding of the other principles.

I define emotion as *a thought attached to a feeling*. Both thoughts and feelings are forms of energy. When we are centered and at peace, we allow thoughts to flow freely through our minds and feelings to flow freely through our bodies. When we disrupt the free flow of thoughts and feelings, we create an energy block that we feel as discomfort.

How do we attach a thought to a feeling, thereby disrupting our energy flow? By labeling, describing, defining, interpreting or judging the feeling. The truth is that feelings aren't subject to interpretation or judgment. Feelings just are. They are like colors on an artist's canvas. There is no objective standard for colors, and one color is not more beautiful, more meaningful or better than another. Colors just are. When they occur together, colors provide a contrast for each other.

So it is with feelings. One is not good and another bad, nor is one more important than another. However, when we intrude on the free flow of feelings by judging them and assigning them values, we create an energy block. Descriptions, evaluations and interpretations of feelings, whether of a positive or negative nature, have the same effect. They stop or distort the flow of feelings through the body.

There is no limit to the range of feelings that we can experience. Part of the beauty of life is to enjoy all the feelings we have. The varied circumstances of our lives give us the opportunity to experience many different kinds of feelings.

Looked at another way, feelings are vibrations of energy. We can become sensitive to all the various shades of vibrations and the various intensities of them. The only impediment to the full enjoyment of each and every vibration is the thinking process. Free of any interpretation, description or evaluation, the vibration of every feeling is enjoyable. When we intervene in the process with our thinking minds, we create an energy block, and thus discomfort, in our bodies.

The availability of sophisticated equipment has enabled scientists to shed light on this matter. When scientists wire subjects to instruments that monitor heartbeat, pulse, respiration, body temperature and other physiological responses, and then induce emotional reactions in the subjects, the scientists find that totally opposite emotional states produce similar physiological responses. What a person calls fear, for example, produces the same responses in his body as what he calls excitement.

Such experiments show us how inaccurate our interpretations of our feelings really are. We generally give a feeling its identity based on the context in which the feeling occurs. When we are at a funeral service, we describe our feelings as sad or grievous. At a wedding or birthday party, we identify our feelings as happy. When preparing to take an examination, we might label our feelings as anxious.

Our interpretation of our feelings is totally subjective and, as demonstrated by the scientists, bears no consistent relationship to the physiological responses in our bodies. In short, we make it up as we go along.

When we interpret a situation as being less than perfect the way it is, we label our feelings accordingly and simultaneously block the flow of energy. When we release the interpretation and the label, we allow the energy of the feeling to flow freely through us. This prompts our natural state of being to come forth—our joyfulness.

By allowing ourselves to accept the inherent perfection of the Universe and all that flows from It, we open ourselves to joyfulness. Experiencing life in the context of joyfulness puts everything in its true perspective. It also brings us into total alignment with our real selves and with everything in the Universe.

❧   ❧   ❧

Question: Do you mean to say that feeling sad or angry is not appropriate under any circumstances?

Answer: Let me first clarify something about feelings. Whatever you are feeling, it is important to allow yourself to feel it fully. However, your characterization of your feeling as angry or sad actually prevents you from feeling the feeling. As long as you are describing the feeling, you are not feeling it. You are feeling a distortion of the feeling.

When you are able to feel your feelings free of any descriptions or interpretations, you are in touch with your true feelings. In the following chapter, I'll present a simple three-step exercise that will assist you in feeling your feelings just the way they are.

But getting back to your question, if someone close to you contracts an illness, such as cancer or AIDS, a feeling other than peacefulness seems appropriate. However, if you can connect to the principle of perfection, you can support yourself, and your friend, by realizing that there is a purpose for everything, although our thinking minds may not understand what that purpose is.

Disease invariably suggests a blocking of energy, a withholding of love—the two are the same. For example, someone may still be angry at his parents for the way he was raised or for some particular incident he believes was unforgivable. He may prefer to retain his anger than to move beyond his judgment of his parents as inadequate or bad. As long as he chooses to remain angry, he is withholding love, not only from his parents but from himself. It is a lack of self-love that allows the disease process to take hold and then advance.

When you are in the presence of the other person, and you are able to feel the inner peace that comes from knowing that the Universe always functions perfectly (despite outward appearances to the contrary), you inspire that person to connect with his own inner peacefulness. This may lead the person to let go of his anger and begin to feel love for his parents, which means he has finally begun to feel love for himself.

❧   ❧   ❧

Question: You say that joyfulness is our natural state of being. Do you really expect people to be joyful at a funeral?

Answer: This is a great question that I am always eager to answer. Funerals represent a series of misperceptions about how the Universe operates. In truth, no one ever dies. Our essence, our real self, is eternal. Beyond the basic misperception about death is the idea that a person is not entitled to choose when to leave her physical body.

Infinite Intelligence granted free will for all. What right do any of us have to tell another person what to do or what not to do? And where do we draw the line? Will you allow me to tell you what color shirt to wear, what kind of food to eat, or what model car to drive? Why should a person's spouse, children or friends be able to tell the person that he cannot leave his body at a particular time? How is this different from limiting his behavior in any other way? Doing so is an infringement on personal freedom.

Society creates the sadness around funerals. Since no one ever really dies, and since we can, if we choose, maintain contact with those who have left their bodies, why all the trauma? When a person leaves on a cruise, we throw a party. A funeral can be like that— celebrating a trip that is certainly more exotic than any cruise.

Funerals have the potential to be gatherings where people can come together to feel the intensity of their feelings, feel their connectedness, and thus feel their deepest joyfulness.

13

THE FEELING EXERCISE

As discussed in the previous chapter, emotions are feelings distorted by the thoughts that we have attached to the feelings. These thoughts include beliefs that it is dangerous to feel and express our feelings. They also include beliefs that it is dangerous to feel and use the power that lies within our feelings.

The process of reconnecting to our feelings and to the power that resides in them calls for a high level of intention. For in order to feel our feelings free of the fears that induced their suppression, and free of the beliefs that distorted them, we have to be willing to first feel our feelings just the way they are—distorted as they may be and fearful as they may seem. The Feeling Exercise supports this process simply and eloquently.

The Feeling Exercise

Close your eyes and scan your body. Notice how you are feeling. Then:

1. Feel the feeling free of any thoughts you have about it. Feel the energy, the power, in the feeling.
2. Feel love for the feeling just the way it is. Feel love for the power in the feeling.
3. Feel love for yourself feeling the feeling and feeling the power in the feeling.

As you begin the process of feeling your feelings free of labels, descriptions or judgments, first notice the *energy* in the feeling. The energy has a *vibration*; feel the energy vibrate through your body. Then notice the *intensity* of the energy as it vibrates through your body. Finally, feel this intensity of energy as *power*—your own power.

We have trained ourselves to repress some very intense feelings for a long time. Be patient with yourself as you begin a new relationship with your feelings—one of appreciation for the vitality and variety they add to your life as you free them from captivity.

It is the labeling of our feelings—as sad, angry, fearful, or whatever—that holds the energy within them and causes us discomfort. As we are able to let go of the labels, we gradually become more comfortable with the return of our power and begin to enjoy the process of feeling our feelings.

Each and every feeling in its undistorted form and free of fear is some aspect of joyfulness. Joyfulness has many aspects. It can be inspiring and entertaining, contemplative and calm, compassionate and caring, or persuasive and compelling. There is no limitation to the range of attributes joyfulness has.

As we practice feeling our feelings just as they are, we increase our trust in ourselves and in others. Eventually, with continued practice, we are able to feel all of our feelings fully, freely and without fear or distortion. Then we shall recognize that every feeling is essentially joyful and a way of deeply connecting to the essence of everyone.

Life is a feeling experience. We feel through our hearts. When we let go of judgments and open our hearts, we give ourselves the joy of feeling all the ways that we love ourselves, others and the world around us. When we open our hearts, we also gain access to the beauty, the aliveness, the wonder and the inspiration that life is.

Question: I can appreciate the value of feeling feelings, but I have a hard time connecting to mine. It seems to me a very threatening process. Can you address this?

Answer: We have all repressed many of our feelings, because we learned at an early age that it is unsafe to express them fully and freely. When we repressed our feelings, we also repressed the power that resides in them. Therefore, whenever we believe it is unsafe or inappropriate to freely feel our feelings, we block our power.

We each have a desire deep within us to reclaim and express our power. As this desire increases, our repressed feelings come to the surface. This is a scary process because the fear that induced the original repression comes to the surface along with the desire to feel the feelings. Yet, as long as we remain too afraid to fully and freely feel our feelings and the power contained within them, we will find ourselves involved in increasingly intense situations that reflect the intensity of our feelings.

Our lives are filled with these outer conflicts. Family quarrels, breakups in marriages, illnesses, legal disputes, wars and an infinite number of other situations are there to show us the intensity of our repressed feelings.

As we practice the Feeling Exercise, which helps us to feel our repressed feelings and to release the energy locked in them, we gradually reduce the need for these outer conflicts. Regular use of this exercise is the most expedient way to fulfill our desire to reclaim our power.

One other point about the Feeling Exercise I want to stress: You will support yourself most effectively if you begin practicing the exercise at times when you are *not* feeling very intense feelings. I suggest that you go through the three steps of the exercise first thing in the morning, last thing at night, and as many times during the day as you can remember. As soon as you notice the least discomfort— either physical or emotional—take a moment to go through the Feeling Exercise. Eventually, you will do it automatically, and you will find yourself feeling all your feelings as pure joyfulness and love.

It feels like a good time to take another break.

SECTION THREE

AWARENESS

14

CAUSE AND EFFECT

If there is one principle that raises more questions and has more built-in resistance to its acceptance than any other, it is the principle of cause and effect. This resistance is unfortunate, because acceptance of the principle brings with it the empowering realization that we are not at the effect of the circumstances in our lives.

The principle of cause and effect tells us that we are the creators of these circumstances. And we create these circumstances with great purposefulness.

The creation occurs at two levels. At one level, cause is put into motion by Infinite Intelligence, God, our essence. We create at this level when we are in a state of peacefulness, when we feel our sense of Oneness, and when we trust in our Infinite Intelligence to guide and support us.

At another level, cause is set in motion by our thinking minds. What we believe creates our experiences.

Under the principle of free will, we are free to believe anything we wish. And our thinking minds are well trained to adopt beliefs as fast as we are taught them.

Whenever our thinking minds override Infinite Intelligence and create out of our beliefs, we receive a signal in the form of discomfort. The signal of discomfort is a reminder that by accepting a belief, we have vested our power in someone or something outside of us.

To put all of this into perspective, it is important to be aware that we are each volunteers who knowingly agreed to accept the beliefs taught to us by our parents and other authority figures. Having accepted and integrated these beliefs, we created the precise circumstances in which we find ourselves.

Some of these circumstances are very intense and challenging. For example, some of us are constantly struggling to survive from day to day, others are in abusive relationships, and still others are battling serious illnesses. Furthermore, many of us have come to our present challenging circumstances from childhood experiences that were equally challenging, such as extreme poverty, child abuse, divorce or alcoholism.

Our agreement to enter into the particular circumstances in which we find ourselves, however, is very purposeful. We took on these beliefs so that we could open the energy around them and thus move ourselves and all who joined with us beyond the limitations created by our beliefs.

Although we may have forgotten that we made such an agreement, it is helpful to realize that we made it knowing that we had the full and continuous support of our Infinite Intelligence. We also knew that with this loving support, we could reclaim the power we vested in whatever circumstances we created. Moreover, we knew that we would have additional powerful support in the form of each other.

The Universe *is* a mutual support system. And though we have avoided following this model in the past, we are now ready to avail ourselves of it. The growth of support groups of all kinds is evidence of both our need for each other's support and our recognition that this support works. In fact, we are now learning that when we join together in mutual support, there is no limit to our power, our creativity and our desire to support one another.

The Belief in Victims and Perpetrators

One of the most widespread beliefs in our society is the belief in victims and perpetrators, and the outplaying of this belief occurs in a vast assortment of circumstances, some of them highly dramatic. Yet whenever we are willing to expand our vision enough to see and feel the essence of everyone who is involved in these circumstances, an event that we previously viewed in terms of victim and perpetrator becomes an opportunity to demonstrate unconditional love and mutual support. As we focus on our Oneness rather than on separation, we become vehicles for transformation of consciousness.

Our willingness to go beyond our beliefs in victims and perpetrators, which we do by opening our hearts, prepares us to reclaim the power we had vested in the people and circumstances outside of us. We no longer need to feel like victims waiting to be victimized by parents, employers, government officials, or just random events such as automobile collisions, diseases and earthquakes.

Once we have reclaimed our personal power, we feel a sense of peacefulness, which frees the creative energy of our Infinite Intelligence. The circumstances we create from this place of peacefulness and divine guidance, then, are not about victims and perpetrators but unconditional lovers and mutual supporters.

❧   ❧   ❧

Question: This is a hard concept for me to accept. If we are the cause of every circumstance in our lives, how can you possibly account for events like rape, murder, or the millions who die in war every day?

Answer: Every event is a reflection of either the individual or group consciousness or both. In the case of the events you mention, the intense hatred, anger and resentment held by many on our planet fuels a seemingly endless cycle of alienation, attack and retaliation.

All participants in such events are in fact loving volunteers who agreed to act out the intense feelings that all of our judgments have repressed. Such events will continue until enough people open their hearts and replace their judgments with compassion and forgiveness, at which time the events on the planet will begin to reflect the deep love we feel for one another.

To answer your question from another vantage point, one of the assumptions you make is that death of the physical body is bad, that dying is a terrible mistake. The most relevant information we have on the subject comes from people who have had what are called near-death experiences. The consensus from the thousands of people who have reported on these experiences is that life without a physical body is wonderful.

In view of this consensus, is it reasonable to conclude that a person who chose to make such a transition was in error? There can be a purpose for staying and a purpose for leaving. No one can know the reason for another's choice. To say, "But she was in the prime of her life, in good health; she had everything to live for" cannot stand up against deeply personal reasons known only to the inner self of the person—reasons that relate to the higher issues of life purpose and reclaiming of power and expansion of consciousness.

I have an observation based on years of experience with many people: Those who accept the law of cause and effect and live by it experience remarkable improvement in the quality of their lives. These people say, "Yes, I am willing to accept that I am the creator of all the circumstances in my life as a way to acknowledge my own power."

I have also observed that those who focus on extreme situations and insist that these events are exceptions to the law of cause and effect, who persist in seeing life in terms of victims and perpetrators, are the same people who deny their personal power and thus forego every opportunity to reclaim it. The result is that they remain the victims that their beliefs convince them they are.

For those who still have doubts about the law of cause and effect, I have a suggestion: Assume that it is the truth. There is no way that you can hurt yourself, for if the law does exist, you gain the benefit of accepting it, and if it doesn't, you lose nothing.

Not accepting the principle of cause and effect means that you are at the mercy of events and can be a victim at any time. This encourages you to continue to believe that you are powerless. If you test the validity of the principle, you will give yourself the chance to reclaim your power and use it to create a truly fulfilling life.

∞ ∞ ∞

Accepting the principle of cause and effect is likely to come easier for those who have developed a loving and trusting relationship with Infinite Intelligence, or God. The next chapter asks you to look more deeply at that relationship.

15

OUR RELATIONSHIP
WITH GOD

What are your feelings about God? Do you accept that God or an Infinite Intelligence is the ultimate creative force for human life and everything else in the Universe? If your answer is yes, do you feel that this Higher Intelligence is unconditionally loving and supportive at all times?

It is important to be aware that the way you relate to the essential energy of the Universe is the way you will experience life. If you honestly accept that God is totally loving and supportive of everyone and everything, under all circumstances, then you will experience a life of total peace and joy. The extent to which your beliefs intrude on this acceptance is the extent to which your life will be less than totally joyful.

There are those who believe that it is better to focus on a concept other than God to explain the creation of the Universe. When a person attempts to avoid the concept of God because thoughts about God bring up feelings of discomfort, then the avoidance will not relieve the discomfort.

As long as we harbor any thoughts that God is less than a totally loving and supportive energy, such thoughts will stand in the way of our feeling the peace of mind and joy that we wish to feel. These same thoughts will lead us to view ourselves and others as less than totally loving and supportive. On the other hand, when we see and feel the perfection and unconditional love of God, we see and feel these same qualities in ourselves and other people.

Our relationship with Infinite Intelligence is the mirror image of our state of consciousness, which can be either free of or limited by our beliefs. This is a simple yet powerful concept that I will address in the next chapter. Given the magnitude of our relationship with God, then, it is to our great advantage to learn to see and feel everyone and everything as a perfect expression of God, for in doing so we see ourselves that way and life becomes that way for us.

Stated in simplest terms, when God becomes our friend, so does everyone else.

We Are One

In developing a good relationship with God, it is helpful to understand that God is not a separate entity, but a unified holistic energy that encompasses everyone and everything in the Universe. We not only are part of this energy, we *are* this energy. Therefore, in the truest sense, we are all One. When we accept this truth, Oneness becomes our experience, and joyfulness becomes our way of life.

We can be certain to feel joyful when we are giving or receiving unconditional love and support, and this will never change. Being loving and supportive is natural to us and the solution to all of our problems.

The energy of love and support that is God, our Oneness, is ever available to us. I experience this support as my Inner Self. In order to feel the connection to my Inner Self, I simply open myself to It and trust that It is, indeed, supporting me.

16

THE MIRROR PRINCIPLE

We have compared life to a game. Another way to view life is to see it as a classroom. This classroom is quite different from traditional ones with walls, designated times of attendance, and individual instructors who teach specific lessons.

This expanded classroom is in session at all times and in all places. The teachers include everyone and everything we interact with. And the lessons are ongoing.

Our all-encompassing classroom provides us with the most efficient and effective means to teach us who we are and what life is all about. Nothing is excluded from the curricula, the subject matter is infinite, and there is no playing hookey. Wherever we are, whatever we are doing, we are in this classroom.

There is a dynamic principle that applies to this classroom, which I call the mirror principle. It states: *Everything that we see and feel is a reflection of the state of our own consciousness.*

What does this principle mean in more concrete terms? Every person that we see is showing us some aspect of who we are. Every thing that we come in contact with reflects to us something about ourselves we might not know. Every feeling that is felt or expressed by another mirrors a feeling deep within each of us.

Our classroom is a veritable hall of mirrors, and while the idea of being surrounded by mirrors might seem outlandish or even nightmarish at first glance, the principle is actually a gift of the highest order. For there is no greater teaching method than demonstration, and the more we learn about ourselves, the greater value our lives have.

As we see ourselves surrounded by mirrors at all times, we realize that whatever is going on is just our state of consciousness being reflected back to us. And our state of consciousness is an accurate reflection of how much love we feel for ourselves.

We are always having an experience with ourselves even though others may be involved. This is a tricky concept to accept. But when we are able to appreciate the concept, our lives will become simpler, and we will also find it easier to feel love for ourselves as well as for others.

I see the Universe as the ultimate teacher. It teaches us directly, consistently and accurately. The mirror principle is the Universe's teaching tool. When we understand how this principle works and use it to our benefit, we graduate to an advanced level of universal education.

❧   ❧   ❧

In order to use the mirror principle in the most beneficial way, there is another principle that is important to understand. This is the principle of nonjudgment, a corollary to the principle of perfection.

17

———— ■ ————

NONJUDGMENT

Our society, which puts such a high value on rational thinking, has carefully taught us to evaluate and judge virtually everything we experience. From the casual "How are you?" to the more deliberate request for some specific appraisal, we are called upon continuously to analyze and criticize just about everyone and everything we interact with. So ingrained is this training that we feel incomplete when we haven't processed each experience in this way.

Yet judging or evaluating anyone or anything inhibits our ability to respond to the essence of the person or thing, which is always perfect. Our judgments also lock in energy.

The moment we evaluate or judge, these limited thoughts attach to our feelings about the person, thing or circumstance. This attachment of a thought to a feeling creates an energy block that causes us discomfort. As long as we hold on to the judgment, the uncomfortable relationship with the person or circumstance keeps replaying itself.

The truth is, there is no such thing as right or wrong, good or bad. Everything that occurs is just another event. By judging something, it becomes for us the way we judge it. The only way to experience the inherent perfection of anything is to see and feel the perfection of it just the way it is.

Let's consider the following example: You cut your finger. If you view the event as bad and become angry at yourself for your carelessness, you miss the whole point. The fact that your finger hurts when you cut it is wonderful. This clear signal from the Universe helps you keep your fingers intact. The pain also tells you that there is a part of you (obviously on an unconscious level) from which you are withholding love. The knowing part of you is calling this to your attention to encourage you to feel more love for yourself.

Having our awareness heightened is most important, for until we are aware of something, it remains the way it is. Pain, which is a strong signal from the knowing part of us to pay attention, can be used in many self-supportive ways. For example, at a support group meeting, you can ask for support in consciousness to pay more attention to the ways you do and do not love and support yourself.

As another example, you can go through the three steps of the Feeling Exercise as a way of moving beyond the pain, beyond the beliefs and patterns that created the pain, to the underlying feeling. The underlying feeling holds the key to the resolution of any self-destructive tendencies you may have, as well as to the release of the pain.

The process works in this way: When you feel the feeling free of the beliefs you have connected to the feeling, you free the energy that is bound up in the feeling. It is the bound-up energy that you feel as pain.

The beliefs we hold are typically the interpretations we made of events that occurred in our lives, usually at an early age. Many of these interpretations were that a particular behavior by a parent or other caretaker was not unconditionally loving and supportive. We might, for example, have been crying in our cribs because we were wet, and our parents, who were involved with other tasks, told us to be quiet instead of changing our diapers.

As infants and children, all of whom are highly sensitive feeling beings, we readily interpreted many actions by our parents and other authority figures as unloving or even cruel. We felt angry and hurt by what we interpreted as uncaring or intentionally abusive behavior. Many of us are still carrying this hurt and anger. And there is a part of us that wants to get even before we give up our anger.

What we did not realize at the time we made the interpretations, and what those of us who are still angry do not realize yet, is that anger is always self-directed, even though we think it is directed at another. Whenever we find fault with anyone, we are really resonating with some aspect of ourselves that we have not yet accepted. Our willingness to cease judging others parallels our willingness to accept ourselves just the way we are. Stated another way, when we are at peace with everyone and everything, then we are at peace with ourselves. We make peace with others to create peace within ourselves.

And how do we make peace with someone for whom we hold strong judgments? We begin with the Feeling Exercise, which, by opening up the energy around our feelings, makes it easier for us to release the angers and resentments we hold. At the same time, we practice feeling forgiveness for the person and continue feeling forgiveness until the angers, resentments and desires for retaliation have abated. We then deepen the feeling of forgiveness until we can feel love for the person, and we focus on the love until it expands into deep love. (See the Forgiveness Exercise on pages 137-38.)

When we feel forgiveness for another, we are really feeling forgiveness for a part of ourselves. When we feel love for another, we are really expressing love for ourselves. We can never escape the fact that we are all deeply loving beings whose greatest joy and most natural way of relating is to feel and express deep love in support of one another.

❧   ❧   ❧

Question: I was abused as a child. Do you really mean to say that child abuse is not bad?

Answer: As hard as it may be for you to accept, the variable that determines how you perceive any event—be it child abuse, rape, murder, or whatever—is not the presence or absence of the event but your interpretation of it.

Are you willing to consider that you are a volunteer who agreed to become part of a particular family for the precise purpose of someday opening the very compacted and painful energies associated with child abuse? If you are willing to accept this as your purpose, you give yourself the opportunity to reclaim all of the power you have vested in your parents and other authority figures.

For those of us exploring the many ways to be in physical form, a favorite excursion is to see how much pain we can tolerate. A variation on this excursion is to create intense pain so that the pleasure, when it comes, seems by contrast that much more intense.

Parents who inflict pain on their children feel the pain themselves. The desire to be free of the pain can inspire either the parent or the child to be the catalyst for transformation by letting go of judgments. This raises the vibrational level of all participants, which creates more space within the body and less density to hold on to the pain.

The release of judgments attached to feelings also frees the energy locked up in the feelings. The power reclaimed from this freed-up energy then becomes available to create more loving and supportive family experiences.

Question: In terms of the principle of nonjudgment, how do you view our criminal justice system?

Answer: Our criminal justice system is a perfect example of how our beliefs in right and wrong, good and bad, reflect back to us individually and collectively.

As an individual, if I believe that I can become a victim at any time, I will very likely create a circumstance in which someone will take the role of victimizer to help me substantiate my belief. People who do not accept themselves as victims do not create circumstances to support that role.

As a society, we see the outplaying of the dominant belief in victims and perpetrators every day in our newspapers and on television. We also see the outplaying of the belief that incarceration and punishment deter criminals. This latter belief is so strong that most people overlook the growing body of evidence showing that crime actually increases as incarceration and punishment increase.

The persistence of this belief in the face of such strong evidence to the contrary further demonstrates that beliefs are not released through a rational process. Beliefs are so tenacious because they are connected to feelings. The power in the belief is in the feeling that is attached to it. Therefore, our willingness to feel our feelings, free of the thoughts and judgments attached to them, is how we shall reclaim the power we have vested in criminals, prosecutors, judges, jailers and all the other components of our criminal justice system.

This system currently has so much of our power that we feel overwhelmed by it. We shall not begin the process of reclaiming our power until we realize that this power is ours to claim and until we love ourselves enough to feel entitled to benefit from this power.

18

TIME

Our society has taught us that time occurs in three stages: the past, the present and the future. In fact, there is only one time that is real—the present. Only the present moment ever really exists.

Our concept of time has a strong impact on our perception. We tend to see our present circumstances in the light of past experiences. In other words, we expect things to remain pretty much the same as they have always been. This is especially true of the way we respond to people. We draw conclusions about the people we interact with, and the next time we are with them we expect them to behave in accordance with our preconceived beliefs about them.

Consider the following example: You are walking down the street and meet a friend who introduces you to the person he is with. This person is obviously impatient and pays little attention to you after she is introduced. While you talk to your friend for a few minutes, the other person waits politely but is obviously growing more impatient and is eager to leave. You next meet this person at a party. As soon as you see her, you remember how impatient she was. Your judgment of her intrudes upon your readiness to find out what she is really like.

You were not aware that when you first met this person, she had just come from visiting her mother, who was critically ill. She was eager to discuss certain decisions about her mother's treatment with her friend. Without realizing it, you were delaying that discussion.

Having drawn certain conclusions about a person, we thereafter expect the person to act in accordance with these conclusions. Our expectation about how she will act encourages her to act that way. Seeing the present through the eyes of the past distorts our view of the present. Consciously or subconsciously remembering how a person behaved previously hampers our ability to relate to the perfection of that person in the present.

It's like comparing a sunset we are currently viewing with the one we saw last night. Each sunset is unique. Comparing tonight's sunset with last night's detracts from our ability to fully experience the sunset we are viewing. In fact, describing it in any way limits our ability to enjoy it fully, for in describing the sunset, we move from our sensory organs, which are responding to its beauty, to our intellects. When we lead with our minds, we bypass our hearts. And it is through our hearts that we feel and enjoy the beauty of life.

Learning to be totally in the present—the only time that ever exists—is a skill that requires consistent practice. We have to remind ourselves continually that whatever we are presently experiencing is unique. It has never happened before, and it will never happen again. We are free to see and feel the present moment in a way we never saw or felt it before.

Remember, perfection cannot be experienced as a thought. It can only be felt. How do we feel another person's perfection? By opening our hearts to that person. Our hearts are our most valuable asset. They are our source of truth, wisdom, peace and joy. There is nothing we cannot heal with an open heart.

❧   ❧   ❧

Question: I can appreciate the value of being in the present moment. But our society lives by the clock. We concern ourselves with getting to work on time, completing jobs on time, and meeting people on time. How do you suggest we learn to relate to clock time in a new way?

Answer: Whenever time appears to be a problem for us, we can be sure we are looking at a phony issue. Let me give you a specific example: Assume that your employer wants you to finish a report by a certain date. You think that she hasn't given you enough time. The truth is, when you are truly inspired to do something, ideas flow rapidly and easily. Time literally collapses.

If, for whatever reasons, you feel you can't finish the report on time, you know you really don't want to finish it on time. The discomfort you feel around the time pressure is a signal—a signal that you are withholding love from your employer and from yourself.

People who believe that time is important will create or attract circumstances that are consistent with that belief. Conversely, people who view time as insignificant will not create or attract circumstances where time can cause them discomfort.

Whenever you notice that the issue of time is bringing up feelings of discomfort, begin the Feeling Exercise. Let yourself feel whatever feelings you have without judgment. When you are able to feel love for these feelings and for yourself feeling them, bring into your conscious awareness anyone or anything in your life that is connected to this issue of time—your employer, your job, a particular assignment. As you move into a place of feeling love for your employer, you will be relating to her heart to heart. Not only will your relationship with your employer feel more peaceful, but you will have released the illusion that time is a problem.

The process sounds so simple, you may resist taking it seriously. However, unless you try it and practice the process consistently, you will have no way of knowing its value. The choice is always yours.

19

AWARENESS AND THE PRM

Most of us spend our time responding to descriptions of what is happening rather than to what is really happening. We believe that we can understand the meaning of every occurrence, so we reduce each experience to something that we can describe. The description then becomes a substitute for the experience.

Paradoxically, we can only understand the meaning of life by letting go of the need to understand. The meaning unfolds for us as we allow ourselves simply to be aware of our experiences without describing, analyzing or evaluating them.

Each of us has a built-in mechanism that is designed to respond perfectly to every event and circumstance in our lives. I call it the Perfect Response Mechanism, or PRM. This PRM is brilliant enough to digest food and take nutrients to the cells in order to support our physical bodies. It is the mechanism that enables a fielder to race to where a baseball will be hit, even before his rational mind can know where the ball is going. The PRM can respond to an infinite number of stimuli instantaneously and simultaneously, if we allow the stimuli to reach the mechanism unimpeded.

Every time the rational mind intervenes in any way to label, describe or evaluate a stimulus, the PRM cannot do its job perfectly. It is like having a state-of-the-art calculator and choosing to do our calculations on our fingers.

To simplify the concept of the Perfect Response Mechanism, imagine a tube that goes from your sensory organs (eyes, ears, nose, mouth, skin) at one end of the tube to your PRM at the other end. Picture a hinged flap in the middle of the inside of the tube. The flap represents your rational mind. Every time your rational mind intervenes by describing, analyzing or judging any stimulus, the flap shuts tight, preventing the sensory stimulus from passing through the tube to the PRM.

Whether or not we use it, the PRM is always available. When we use it, its brilliance is immediately evident. My suggestion is to use the PRM as often as possible. This requires that we keep our thinking minds from intervening, which is not always an easy task.

Here are two awareness exercises that can give you a direct experience of how your Perfect Response Mechanism works:

When in your home, select a dominant feature of each room to focus your senses on whenever you enter the room. For example, focus on odors when you go into your kitchen and on colors when you are in your living room. When you first awake, pay attention to the sounds you hear. While you are eating, focus on the texture or taste of each food you ingest.

Make up other exercises that keep your attention focused on something in your immediate environment, and vary the exercises to maintain your interest. When you lose interest, your thinking mind becomes free to intervene, and it will invariably hinder the stimuli from reaching the PRM.

When driving a car or taking a walk, pay attention to the subtle energy changes that take place each time you pass another vehicle or person. Notice the difference in energy between a car passing in your direction and one going in the opposite direction. Notice the difference in energy between passing one person or a group of people or in passing a dog or a tree.

The beauty of these exercises is that the focus on one aspect of the immediate environment enhances the ability of the PRM to receive all other stimuli from that environment. The PRM not only responds perfectly to each stimulus, but its sequence of responses is also perfect.

Let's return to the exercise of driving a car. By focusing your thinking mind on the energy changes as you drive along, you avoid evaluating your experience. Using the visual image of the tube, you keep the flap in its open position, which allows all of the stimuli in your immediate environment to pass directly from your sensory organs to the PRM. Stimuli such as road noises, the smell of fumes, and physical sensations in your body are received by the PRM. The perfect response or sequence of responses is then transmitted to you intuitively. This can lead you to discover another route or to attract a job where the commute runs opposite to the main flow of traffic.

If you allow yourself to evaluate the experience, you are likely to find yourself judging the situation as less than perfect. You may then become irritated at the traffic or annoyed at having to drive to work. Once you evaluate or judge the experience, you inhibit the natural operation of your PRM, and you relinquish your capacity to respond intuitively and joyfully.

Our Perfect Response Mechanism is directly connected to Infinite Intelligence. That is how the PRM knows how to respond perfectly to every situation. If we had no preconceived ideas and beliefs as to how the world worked and, instead, just allowed the Universe to guide us, we would continually experience the beauty of life. What stands in the way are our beliefs and our vested interests, our wanting to have things a certain way.

The awareness exercises suggested in this chapter, as well as the exercises suggested in other chapters, if practiced consistently, can help you to open the energy locked in your beliefs and to reach the state of peace and joy that life is really all about. The more you can experience being in this state, the greater your incentive will be to open the energy around all beliefs that keep you from enjoying life to the fullest.

❧ ❧ ❧

This is a good time to take another break. During the break, you might try playing with one of the exercises—or a variation of it—described in this chapter.

SECTION FOUR

ABUNDANCE

20

ABUNDANCE IS OUR NATURAL STATE

Abundance is the word I use to refer to the infinite expression of energy in the Universe. Mastering abundance means mastering energy, and vice versa.

How do we master abundance? We begin with the following eight steps:

1. Recognize the basic principle.

The basic principle of abundance is that abundance is the natural state of the Universe. Since everything in the Universe is energy, then we know that abundance is energy. Abundance—energy—is all around us and in infinite supply, and it is available to each of us whenever we are open to receive it.

2. Be aware of contradictory beliefs.

The second part of the principle of abundance states that if we are experiencing less than total abundance in each and every aspect of our lives, we can be sure we are resisting the natural flow of abundance. We resist this natural flow by holding on to beliefs that contradict the truth of abundance. The most common of these beliefs are that we have to work hard, earn a living, be productive, achieve a particular lifestyle or gain certain credentials to receive abundance. How many of us believe, for instance, that in order to have as much money as we would like, we have to hold a job we do not enjoy but that pays well? The unhappy result of this belief is that we attract job after job that is unsatisfying to us.

3. Generate intention and commitment.

Our beliefs in shortage and lack are so pervasive that it requires great intention and commitment to allow the truth of our natural state of abundance to permeate our conscious awareness. Without a high level of intention, our deeply held beliefs will continue to have the power to create situations in the physical world that appear to contradict the truth of abundance.

4. Notice your present abundance.

Much of the abundance that we think we desire we already have. Most of us enjoy a remarkable array of abundance in the forms of caring and loving friends to spend time with, nourishing food to eat, wardrobes of clothes to choose from, comfortable housing to live in, a wide variety of transportation to afford us all kinds of travel, entertaining and inspiring books to read, pets to comfort us, flowers to delight us—the list is truly endless. However, our tendency is to take for granted what we already have and to focus on what we do not have.

This leads us to another principle, which we will go into in more detail further in the book, that states: What we focus on expands. By noticing the abundance that we already have, we open ourselves to receive more. By focusing our attention on what we do not have, we actually attract more scarcity.

5. Practice giving generously, receiving gratefully and feeling gratitude for the abundance you have.

If abundance is energy, and all energy is love, then abundance is love. Energy (love) wishes to flow freely and to stay in balance. We support this free flow and balance by giving generously, receiving gratefully, and feeling and expressing gratitude for all that we have. Gratitude opens us to receive love, of which material abundance is but one expression.

6. Remember the principle of cause and effect.

The principle of cause and effect reminds us that the beliefs generated by our thinking minds create the circumstances in which money and other forms of abundance either seem to be absent from our lives, come in only after great effort, or cause chaos when they are present. This same principle also reminds us that our inner knowing, our connection to Infinite Intelligence, which we hear or feel when our thinking minds are quiet, guides us effortlessly and joyfully when we surrender to it.

7. Practice nonjudgment and mutual support.

Our willingness to release the judgments we have around the people and circumstances in our lives frees the energy to flow to us as abundance. Creating mutually supportive and harmonious relationships also helps us to open to the flow of abundance.

8. Be patient with the process.

Mastering abundance, as with mastering energy, is a gradual, step-by-step process. Trust that the process happens at the perfect pace and that staying focused in the present moment is the best way to move the process along. Our inner knowing always presents to us the precise issue we need to deal with at just the appropriate time. Our task is to be sensitive to the guidance of our inner knowing.

As long as the process remains an intellectual exercise, no real movement occurs. We are feeling beings and life is a feeling process. One way we can know we are on the right track is when we are feeling peaceful. Peacefulness is not a state of mind, it is a state of heart. When we are feeling peaceful, we know that we are in our hearts rather than in our heads.

Peacefulness is the door through which we gain access to the abundance of the Universe. It is only in a state of peacefulness that we can feel our Oneness, out of which all abundance flows.

❧ ❧ ❧

Question: If abundance is our natural state, why do so many people struggle so hard to achieve it?

Answer: When our belief is that we have to struggle to attain abundance, and I'll assume you are referring specifically to material wealth, then the only way we'll allow ourselves to have material wealth is by struggling.

For much of my life, I held just that belief. During my twenty-five years of earning a living, I achieved most of my material wealth in less than five percent of the time I devoted to my career. The rest of the time I literally created problems and obstacles to overcome so that the money I received would be properly earned.

After I made the shift to expressing my talent for teaching, I blocked the flow of money. What I didn't realize was that I still had struggle and material wealth wired together in my belief system. I could express my talent, but I couldn't receive money for teaching without struggling. Gradually I have been allowing fun and financial success to join together.

The truth that we always create what is perfect for us to experience cannot be pushed aside or ignored. This principle is in constant operation whether we are aware of it or not. People who struggle to earn a living, disliking what they do, are demonstrating their belief that life cannot be filled with joy and abundance. The demonstration lets them know they have such a belief so that they can reclaim the power they vested in the belief.

There are no surprises in life. We are all open books. We can read our own books, or we can let others read our books for us. Whenever we are ready, we can learn who we are and what we are up to. We can choose to be aware; we can wake up.

We are smarter than we think, and life is simpler than we realize. It is time for us to recognize and appreciate these truths, and to open our hearts to the infinite abundance that is in us and all around us.

21

GIVING AND RECEIVING

The principle of giving and receiving is central to our understanding of abundance and thus of energy. Giving and receiving are two sides of the same coin, and they always occur in balance. To have a completed gift there must be a giver who truly wants to give and a receiver who is truly open to receive.

To understand the concept of giving and receiving, it is important to define the term "giving." True giving fulfills the following three criteria:

1. The giver sincerely wishes for the recipient to have and to enjoy the gift.
2. The gift is something the giver sincerely believes the recipient wishes to have.
3. There are no ulterior motives or strings attached by the giver, and the recipient is free to do with the gift as he wishes.

When a person gives—voluntarily and with no expectations—she creates a vacuum, in a sense, and is now ready to receive. Concurrently, the recipient is in a position to give. It is not necessary that the receiver give something back to the same person who gave to him. The ideal is for both giver and receiver to keep the flow going and allow everything to move freely in and out of their lives. Holding on to anything, developing an attachment to it, blocks the flow. (We'll look more closely at the principle of nonattachment in a later chapter.)

To assist you in integrating the principle of giving and receiving, visualize a circle of people in which each person is giving to and receiving from another person in the circle. When everything is moving freely around the circle, everyone receives the benefit of whatever is circulating, including the energy, which is increasing in its rate of vibration. If even one person holds on to anything, the flow stops, and everyone feels the block in energy as well as the drop in the rate of vibration.

Going back to the most basic principle, what are we really giving when we make a true gift? We are giving energy, or love, which is in infinite supply and is the motivating force within everything in the Universe. Love truly makes the world go round. And by its nature, it keeps expanding.

We Give Only to Ourselves

There is a corollary to the principle of giving and receiving, and that is that we give only to ourselves. Since we are all One, who else is there to give to?

When we give something for the pure pleasure of giving, our feelings of generosity inspire others to be generous. When we feel gratitude for the gifts of love we receive, these feelings raise the vibration of the Oneness that we are, so that everyone and everything feels more joyful. Such are the dynamics behind the principle that we give only to ourselves.

Consider for a moment someone you know or have known who enjoyed giving so much that she was the continual recipient of gifts from others. Many of us know such people. Each of us can become a generous giver when we integrate into our consciousness the truth that we can give only to ourselves.

⚘   ⚘   ⚘

Question: I have two friends—one who is very generous but who is always in debt, and the other who is very wealthy but who holds on to what he has. One seems to give more than he receives and the other seems to receive more than he gives. You said giving and receiving are always in balance. Can you explain this apparent discrepancy?

Answer: We often don't recognize the balance between giving and receiving when money is part of the equation, because we forget that money is not the only form of abundance. Remember that abundance is just energy and therefore includes experiences as well as material wealth. It also includes opposites, such as assets and debts, peacefulness and tension, generosity and hoarding.

Each of us is free to select the form of abundance we give and receive. We make our selections based on the feelings we wish to generate. Each choice is personal and subjective. And the feeling quality each choice generates is of prime importance.

With so many variables, we can see why assessing the balance between giving and receiving can be tricky, particularly when the feeling quality is such an important aspect. Only the person who is involved in the giving and receiving, and is feeling the effects of the balance, can really assess the balance.

However, I'll give a few examples to offer a general idea of how giving and receiving might come into balance in the two situations you presented in your question.

Let's start with the generous person, who seems to give more than he receives. When this person goes into debt, someone else is being generous to him in lending him money. If the borrower can sustain such a situation, it means his credit is good. Those who lend to him are giving him their trust that he will repay them.

The generous person may be receiving something else as well. He may be enjoying the excitement that the tension of being in debt brings. Or he might find that owing money stimulates him to produce dramatic solutions for bringing in the funds to pay the debt.

As for the person who seems to receive more than he gives and who holds on to what he has, this is often someone who believes he needs such a storehouse of material wealth for his own security—to fill a deep feeling of void within. This is generally a person who does not feel much love for himself. From this person's vantage point, the void is so great that what looks like hoarding to an outsider is really felt as an inadequate amount to the recipient. He feels that he needs an ever-increasing amount to keep himself in balance.

Giving and receiving are always in balance in each of us. And only each of us can know and appreciate the elements that make up this balance. How it appears to an outsider is irrelevant. How it is for us is very relevant, and heightened awareness to the feeling quality involved can become the incentive to increase our love for ourselves— the only real variable in the equation of giving and receiving.

Since we have touched on the subject and since it is such a common and growing concern to so many, let's look more closely at the subject of debt.

22

DEBT

For those of us who are challenged by debts, it can be helpful to know that we took on the beliefs, patterns and feelings of a debt consciousness so that we could transform them. And we have a substantial task, for our society is experiencing an expansion of its debt consciousness. Personal debts as well as city, state and federal debts are at an all-time high and climbing.

The concept of debt is a direct outgrowth of our society's extensive reliance on the concept of obligation. We were raised to believe that we are obligated to do many things—pay attention to parents, attend school, obey laws, earn a living, pay taxes, take care of our elders. So much of our life is devoted to doing things out of a sense of obligation that we have developed a strong obligation consciousness. Debt is just another word for obligation. The many debts we create as individuals and as a society are just an outplaying of our obligation consciousness.

Having immersed ourselves in the beliefs, patterns and feelings of an extensive debt consciousness, we are in the perfect position to transform them. In fact, it is only through our willingness to take on the full intensity of these beliefs, as well as the intensity of the circumstances that accompany them, that we can transform these beliefs.

We carry out the transformation of our debt consciousness by first of all reminding ourselves that this is one of the things we came here to do. We then practice seeing and feeling the perfection of each and every debt and obligation that comes into our experience. Next, we do the Feeling Exercise and continue doing it daily until we feel at peace with each debt and with each creditor. The resolution of the debt will emerge from our peaceful feelings about the debt and the creditor. The resolution can come about in many ways, including the funds to pay it or a forgiveness by the creditor.

The discomfort that we feel from having unpaid debts is the signal to proceed with the resolution. When we avoid seeking this resolution, the discomfort intensifies, for our energy flows into our beliefs and feelings all the time, whether we are consciously aware of these beliefs and feelings or not. And this steady flow of energy keeps intensifying whatever is going on.

The opposite of avoidance is awareness. Avoidance intensifies our discomfort. Awareness encourages us to bring to peace whatever is going on around us, including being in debt.

❧   ❧   ❧

Question: I have some trouble with the idea of transforming our debt consciousness. I just feel resentful of those to whom I owe money. Can you offer any insights to give me some support with this?

Answer: It may help you to realize that debt is not the beginning of a transaction; it is invariably the second part. The first part involves receiving something of value, such as money, clothes, a car, a vacation.

If you can see payment of a debt as a gift to a person or company that gave something to you, you might find that repaying a debt is fun. When you give a birthday present to a friend, you feel good. Paying a debt can be similar. When it isn't fun to pay a bill, it means you are withholding love. This awareness can lead you to increase your love both for yourself and for your creditors. As your love expands, so does the flow of abundance.

I encourage you not to be fooled by the simplicity of this idea. When you enjoy paying bills, and that includes paying taxes, you know you are achieving mastery of the principle of abundance.

Question: You explained what we need to do if we are in debt. But what do we do when someone is in debt to us, and particularly if the person is resisting repayment?

Answer: The simplest way to encourage repayment of a loan is to free the borrower of the obligation to repay it. In this way, the repayment becomes voluntary. You are, in effect, saying to the borrower, "It is up to you to decide what you want to do about the money you received from me."

If the borrower ever had the intention to repay you, she is now in a position to feel that intention again. It is your best chance for repayment. Of course, the less you are concerned about whether she ever repays you, the more you set in motion the energy for others, not just the borrower, to give to you. This has to do with the principle of nonattachment, the subject of the next chapter.

23

NONATTACHMENT

Air moves freely through the atmosphere. Water flows freely down a mountain stream. Waves roll freely onto ocean beaches. The earth moves freely on its axis. The nature of life is freedom of movement.

Looked at from the viewpoint of energy, we know that energy requires free movement in order to function effectively and efficiently. The energy of the Universe wants to flow freely around and through us. When we allow it to, we and everyone else benefits. Each time we interfere with this free flow of energy, we reduce, proportionately, the abundance coming to us. Blocking the flow of energy also results in discomfort in our bodies—a signal from the Universe that we are out of alignment with principle.

One of the ways that we interfere with the free flow of energy is by holding on to what we have. We hold on to money or things of material value. We hold on to people with whom we have relationships.

Holding on to anything—people or possessions—blocks the free flow of energy around our experience with the person or object and reduces the pleasure of the experience. It also inhibits new people and new things from coming into our lives.

Having Does Not Require Holding

There is a difference between having something and holding on to it. You can own a house, enjoy it, and feel no attachment to it. Or you can own a house, believe that it represents your security, and fear losing it. The latter is attachment, and it will block the free flow of energy into your life.

You can have a relationship with a person, feel a total commitment to the relationship, trust the other person completely, and yet have no attachment to the person or to the relationship. You give the other person total freedom at all times. The relationship continues as a result of the participants making a moment-by-moment recommitment to the relationship.

By not holding on to a relationship, you allow other people to come into your life. Each relationship has its own kind of commitment that is unique to it, and every relationship adds to the quality of every other relationship. In fact, while we are engaged in one relationship, the energies of our other relationships flow through us to enrich our present experience. If we feel a need to hold on to one or more of our relationships, we block the free flow of energy around all of our relationships.

People tend to hold on to things or to accumulate them when they fear they might not have what they need at some future time.

In other words, they do not trust the natural abundance of the Universe to provide them with the appropriate things at the perfect time.

When we do not trust the Universe to function perfectly, It reciprocates. The Universe always gives us what we believe, whether that is shortage or abundance. At the same time, however, It also gives us clear signals, which we feel in the form of discomfort, to let us know that we have chosen other than the joy of abundance.

There is another reason people tend to hold on to things. We believe that we know better what we need than Infinite Intelligence, or God. This belief is based on the misperception that God is separate and distant from us and is less than totally loving and supportive at all times. Trusting that God is not only there for us but *is* us is key to enjoying all the gifts of this loving and supportive energy.

If each of us were trusting enough to put more of what we own into circulation, imagine how much more of everything there would be for everyone to share and enjoy! Remember that there is an infinite supply of energy available to everyone at all times. The only shortage we ever experience is the result of our belief that some things are in short supply or not available to us. What we are dealing with is a perception of shortage, not a real shortage.

Mastering nonattachment requires the willingness to accept that the Universe is a place of total abundance. Until we arrive at this acceptance, we will continue to create circumstances that validate what we believe. When we finally recognize that abundance is our natural state, we release all attachment to material abundance so that it is free to flow into our lives.

ை   ை   ை

Question: You used the word "security" in reference to owning a home. It seems to me that most people would agree that owning a home makes them feel secure. I'm not sure I see what's wrong with that.

Answer: There's nothing wrong with wanting to feel secure, but we buy into an illusion when we believe that owning a home is the way to accomplish this.

Security is not something that we attain outside of ourselves. In fact, the person who looks to create a feeling of security by accumulating assets or amassing material wealth is actually working against himself, because all of his efforts are going toward reinforcing a misperception and undermining the truth.

The truth is that the Universe is always in total support of everyone. We feel secure when we know this to be true. Any time we choose to create a feeling of security by buying more things or by increasing our net worth, we are vesting our power in things and money and thus increasing our feeling of insecurity. This deepens our mistrust in our true security, which comes only from trust in the inherent safety and abundance of our Universe.

Question: To master nonattachment, is it necessary to give up all our assets and everything we own?

Answer: Not at all. Having something and owning it are two different things. We cannot truly own anything in the Universe. Nothing really belongs to us.

There is common agreement in our society on various forms of ownership, be it houses or cars, children or pets. We are led to believe that we can own things; in fact, we are encouraged to hold this belief. Furthermore, most of us were taught that success means ownership of many things.

However, ownership contradicts the concept of freedom of movement. The only way to truly enjoy anything is to let it be free to move. If you allow a thing to be free, and it chooses to stay around, you know that it is perfect for you to have and enjoy. If the thing leaves, you know that there is something else that is perfect for you to have and enjoy.

Letting go in order to have is a concept that requires a lot of practice. Letting go does not mean you have to divest yourself of everything. This is strictly a perceptual issue. It means letting go of the perceived need to own or hold on to anything.

My suggestion is that you continue to practice releasing your attachment to things and people until you feel peaceful whether the object or person is there or not. One of the great benefits of reaching this state of peacefulness is that you will not feel so disappointed or sad when the object or person is gone.

The principle of nonattachment is a direct corollary to the principle of abundance. When we accept the natural flow of abundance, we know that no matter what we give up, there is an infinite supply of energy available to replace it.

In discussing abundance, we inevitably focus on *things* in the material world—money, objects, people. But abundance can also take the form of the many talents we have to share and enjoy.

24

———— ■ ————

EXPRESSING WHO WE ARE

O ne of the ways the Universe expresses Its infinite love and abundance is through Its gift to each of us of one or more talents. Knowing where our talents lie and being willing to express them is key to releasing our inner joyfulness.

We do not learn a talent; it is inherent within us. Moreover, each talent comes complete with the tools to express it perfectly. For example, if you have an artistic talent, you have all the skills necessary to express your particular art form in the perfect way.

What determines how successful a person will be at expressing her unique talent or talents is how much love she feels for herself. Self-love is always the starting point. When you love yourself, you not only acknowledge your talent, you delight in practicing and expressing it. Furthermore, by giving voice to your talent consistently, you uncover more of your talent and you gain confidence and comfort in expressing it more freely and fully. You also give yourself the plea-sure of refining the talent through consistent practice and expression.

Expressing a talent is not a rational-mind activity. As artists or musicians or dancers, we do not think about what colors to select or notes to play or movements to make. We allow ourselves to be totally intuitive, letting the infinite supply of creative energy move freely through us. We release any sense of limitation. The activity is one of freedom and joy, not thought and effort.

When we are able to move beyond our beliefs in limitation and open to the infinite supply of energy in the Universe, extraordinary things happen—different and unique for each person. Expressing our talents fully and freely leads us to feel our perfection, so that our perfection expands. We shall fly into joy whenever we are ready to untie our wings.

Discovering Our Talents

The way we each discover our inherent talent is to notice what brings us the most joy and fulfillment when we express ourselves. What gives us joy is what we have a natural talent to express. The following exercise will help you to discover what talent you most love to express right now:

Make a list of those activities you most enjoy, the ones that inspire you at the mere thought of them. The feeling of in-spiration is more important than the number of activities on your list. In fact, the shorter the list, the more effective the exercise will be.

Select the one activity on the list that most inspires you. You may feel resistance to choosing only one activity, but understand that picking one does not mean you have to give up the others forever.

Now make a list—this time as long as you want it to be— of all the ways you might express the talent you selected in the previous step. Allow the ideas to come to you spontaneously and without judgment. Write down every idea, regardless of how silly or trivial it might seem to you. The purpose of the exercise is to stimulate your creativity.

I suggest you write the ideas in a separate notebook and add to the list every day. After doing the exercise over a period of time, you will develop a habit pattern of coming up with creative ways to express your talent.

The number of ways you can express your talent has no limit. Using your creativity to produce these ideas is one way to experience the abundance of the Universe.

We all know where our talents lie. This knowledge is an integral part of us. We can, however, keep the information from ourselves as a way to withhold love from ourselves. The beauty of our perfect Universe is that we can approach the issue from either direction: We can develop our feelings of self-love so that we allow ourselves to express our talents, or we can express our talents as a means of expanding our self-love.

The pleasure that comes from expressing our talents is a deep, fulfilling pleasure, for in expressing our talents, we are expressing who we really are. And who we are is the perfect expression of God, our Oneness.

ॐ   ॐ   ॐ

Question: I have a hard time picking just one activity I love. There are many ways I love to express myself. Can't I have them all?

Answer: Eventually, yes, you can. But you want to start with just one activity. This relates to the efficient use of energy. The more you focus your energy on one activity, the more power that activity will have. Once you achieve success with one activity, you can move on to another.

There are many multitalented people. The ones who are the most successful are the ones who started by focusing their attention on one talent and then went on to focus on another. By giving just a little of our attention to several activities, we scatter our energy and make it almost impossible to enjoy any of our talents at any real level of success. The dilettante syndrome is well known.

If you look at the life of a recognized superstar, you will notice that most of the things the superstar does are very ordinary. He or she is perceived as a superstar for expressing one talent in an outstanding way.

We each have the natural ability to express at least one talent on a superstar level. When we love ourselves enough to recognize what that talent is and then focus our full attention on expressing it, each of us becomes a superstar also.

❧   ❧   ❧

We have already touched on the principle addressed in the next chapter. This is the principle that states: What we focus on expands.

25

WHAT WE FOCUS ON EXPANDS

We are free to focus our attention wherever we wish. We can focus on all that we have, or we can obsess on what we don't have. We can focus on what we perceive to be problems, or we can remind ourselves that everything has a purpose and that every circumstance is an opportunity to reclaim our power.

When we choose to sustain our beliefs in lack and struggle, we support these beliefs with additional thoughts that are consistent with this way of seeing the world. The more we give our attention, or energy, to our beliefs in struggle, the more circumstances we attract to us that substantiate such beliefs.

In fact, we have been in the process of expanding our beliefs about lack and struggle for thousands of years. And we have millions of scenarios—past, present and future—to "verify" the supposed reality of lack and struggle.

So we know the truth of the principle that what we focus on expands. But what we have a more difficult time understanding is how to reverse the process.

If focusing on scarcity results in situations of shortage, why not just focus on abundance? If someone is having challenges around not having enough money, for example, why can't she just focus her attention on lots of cash?

The answer is that there are two parts to the process of focusing attention, not just one, as most of us have been led to understand. It is not just a matter of focusing our thoughts on what it is we wish to expand. As we have discussed previously, our power lies in our feelings. It is the power in our feelings, which we attach to our thoughts, that fuels the creation of the circumstances in our lives.

Thus, in order to empower our focus on having abundance, we have to shift the feeling attached to the belief in shortage to the willingness to receive abundance. We do this by reclaiming the power we have vested in the belief in shortage and using that power to expand our love for ourselves. We then feel worthy of receiving abundantly from the Universe.

Our willingness to focus on our feelings, then, is the most constructive first step we can take in reclaiming the power we have placed outside ourselves. However, often when we attempt to focus on our feelings, our thinking minds again intercede and interpret for us the meaning of our feelings. As a consequence, although we believe we are feeling our feelings, we are really feeling an interpretation of a feeling. In this subtle way, our thinking minds thwart our desire to connect with our feelings and the power that resides in them.

Our thinking minds are a product of our training, and they function precisely as they were trained to. Our thinking minds keep replaying exactly what they have been taught—beliefs that have been deemed valuable to hold and that we, by agreement with those who taught us these beliefs, have not only accepted but internalized.

To call these beliefs bad or wrong is not helpful. As the principle of nonjudgment reminds us, judging our beliefs only reinforces them by locking up the energy within them. If we wish to move beyond our beliefs, the solution is to quiet our thinking minds and focus our full awareness on our feelings. Our feelings are not only the source of our power, but our access point to our inner knowing, our connection with Infinite Intelligence.

In simplest terms, the principle that what we focus on expands can inspire us to keep our conscious awareness on the real creative force in the Universe—the power in our feelings. When we focus on our pure feelings, unencumbered by beliefs, what expands within us and around us is peace, joy and abundance.

❧　❧　❧

Question: Where do affirmations fit into Universal Principles?

Answer: Affirmations are often used as a means to change our beliefs, and as such, they often have the effect of creating exactly the opposite result of what we have intended. For example, someone who is struggling with illness might repeat the affirmation, "I am strong and healthy."

The difficulty in affirming something that is not consistent with how we presently feel is that the process actually bypasses our place of power—our feelings. Furthermore, with the emphasis on our thinking minds, we are giving importance to the part of us that is reinforcing the very belief that we are trying to override.

The essential first step in dealing with a belief we hold but are uncomfortable with is to accept that we have the belief. The next step is to release judgment of the belief; allow the belief to be perfect just the way it is. This paves the way to do the Feeling Exercise, which extracts the power we have vested in the belief.

We often use affirmations to shore us up when we feel powerless in a world that seems less than supportive and friendly. However, affirmations, as a mental activity, often expand our sense of powerlessness, whereas the Feeling Exercise increases our feeling of power, and thus the world around us appears less threatening.

There is a way to use affirmations that is self-supportive. Choose statements that reflect the highest truth and that inspire you at a deep feeling level. Examples might include: "I am One with God" or "The Universe is safe, friendly and abundant" or simply "I choose love." Let the affirmations come to you, and choose words that are personal to you. If, when you say an affirmation, the statement gives rise to feelings other than peacefulness and joy, do the Feeling Exercise until you feel totally at peace with the words.

When you affirm the truth, you have the support of your Inner Self. As you repeat loving, supportive words, the energy of the words fills your being with loving, supportive feelings.

❧   ❧   ❧

It's time for another break. When you come back, we'll focus on a topic that is at the heart of Universal Principles: our life's purpose.

SECTION FIVE

SELF-LOVE

26

PURPOSE

To master the game of life, there is no more valuable step you can take than to become aware of your life's purpose. When you are able to answer the question, "What is my individual role in the Universe?" you benefit fully from the beauty, power and perfection of our magnificent Universe.

Your awareness of your purpose develops your sense of belonging. It allows you to see yourself as an essential part of a much larger experience. You no longer feel separate or alone.

When you are aware of your purpose, whatever happens to you, viewed within the context of your purpose, appears meaningful. No longer do you see situations as isolated, insignificant events in your life.

Furthermore, if you ask yourself how what you are about to do aligns with your purpose, you can greatly simplify and enhance the quality of your life. You may choose to discontinue doing some things and to spend more time expressing yourself in ways that give you greater satisfaction.

I suggest that you connect with your purpose several times every day. You can read or state it silently or aloud, but more important is to connect with the inspiration you feel when you say your purpose. In this way, you reinforce your realization of your importance in our Universe. You also stay open to the Infinite Intelligence that can guide you in every decision you are called upon to make.

In addition, I suggest that you connect with your purpose whenever something is troubling you. The event or circumstance is perceived as troubling because you are seeing it from a limited view as an isolated event. As you connect with your purpose, you expand your view of the event and begin to see its broader meaning in your life.

Becoming Aware of Your Purpose

To begin the process of becoming aware of your purpose, let yourself grow quiet and go through the three steps of the Feeling Exercise. In a state of deep self-love and peacefulness, ask yourself, "What is my purpose for living?" or "What is my unique role in the Universe?"

Allow the answer to come to you. Let it be as expansive as you can imagine. The words you choose need not be flowery or poetic; what is important is how inspired the words make you feel. Also, the simpler your purpose, the more powerful it will be. Here are some examples of statements of purpose:

> ✨ *My purpose is demonstrating the joy and power of an open heart.*

✕ In a spirit of fun, I inspire wisdom and creative expression.

✕ My purpose is choosing love, joy, freedom and abundance.

✕ In harmony and integrity, I playfully express my love and creativity.

When you connect with your purpose, you invite inspiration into your life. You give yourself permission to express your real self. And you feel the joy that is your essence.

Preparing for Joy and Abundance

Part of the perfection of the Universe is that It provides everyone with both the energy and the motivation to create a life of ever-increasing joy. This gift allows you to fashion a life of such beauty and abundance that you feel grateful in every moment for everything around you.

Here are a few suggestions for preparing the way for more beauty, joy and abundance in your life:

1. Become aware of your purpose and connect with it, at a feeling level, several times every day.
2. Let your sense of the value of your role in the Universe expand.
3. Allow your life to become a joyful expression of being who you are. When you express who you really are, you fulfill your perfect role in the universal scheme.
4. Continually remind yourself of the real game of life and play it as often as you can. When you are living your life in alignment with your purpose and expressing who you really are, you are automatically playing the real game.

5. View every event or circumstance within the context of your purpose and in accordance with Universal Principles. This improves your ability to feel joyful under all circumstances.

6. Be part of a support system that is committed to playing the real game of life (see Section Seven).

❧   ❧   ❧

Question: I don't have a sense of what my purpose is. What should I do about that?

Answer: Everyone has a purpose. Your apparent inability to connect with your purpose is a signal that you are withholding love from yourself. When you let yourself feel your sense of purpose, you give yourself a wonderful gift of inspiration and aliveness. However, you will not allow yourself to receive this gift until you first increase your love for yourself.

The next chapter delves more deeply into the issue of self-love and offers a simple yet powerful exercise to assist you in increasing your love for yourself.

27

SELF-LOVE AND
THE MIRROR EXERCISE

E ach of us is the reference point and the source of everything in our lives. The way we see ourselves and, more importantly, the way we feel about ourselves determines how we experience life. Stated more succinctly, we are always having a relationship with ourselves, regardless of who else or what else is present.

No one and no thing is really separate from us. Our belief in separation is a perceptual distortion, a projection of our unwillingness to love ourselves just the way we are.

What does this mean in practical terms? The more you are willing to feel love for yourself just the way you are, the sooner you will create circumstances that reflect your self-love.

And how do you feel more love for yourself?

The simplest and most powerful way to increase your love for yourself is by doing what I call the Mirror Exercise.

The Mirror Exercise

Stand or sit in front of a mirror. Look at yourself eye to eye.
Go through the three steps of the Feeling Exercise. Continue
looking at yourself until you feel deep love for yourself.

When you look at yourself in a mirror, you quickly learn how you
really feel about yourself. Whatever reasons you have for not accepting yourself the way you are immediately come to your attention. The
receding hairline, the unwanted pounds, the wrinkles, the anger glar-
ing from the eyes, the look of fear or sadness—these are just a few of
the infinite reasons we have for not loving ourselves the way we are.

As you continue to look in the mirror, allow the feelings behind
the reasons to rise to the surface. At the same time, allow your heart
to open and feel love for these feelings. Let the love expand until you
feel love for yourself.

In the beginning, the reasons not to feel love for yourself will
predominate and draw your attention away from the feelings. Keep
returning your focus to your feelings and to feeling love for yourself.
Consider just a small amount of self-love to be a big accomplishment.
Little by little and with persistence, your willingness to feel more love
for yourself increases. And before you realize it, you are feeling a lot
of love for yourself.

Once you have a taste of feeling love for yourself, your life will
never be the same, for you will connect with who you really are. You
will also connect with a hint of how powerful you really are.

There is no limit to how much love for ourselves we can feel, and
there is no limit to the full power of our being. There is, however, a
perceptual barrier—our personal reasons for being unlovable. These

reasons steadily diminish in importance as we persist in reconnecting the energy we placed in them with the deep love we feel for ourselves.

It is important to remember that underneath all of the reasons we have for not loving ourselves resides our true self, our essence, which is pure love. This essence loves us deeply at all times and knows that all of the reasons we have for not loving ourselves are just shallow excuses to hang on to a way of life we were taught and a misguided loyalty to those who taught us.

Who we really are is a powerful force that will not be denied. Just a little willingness is required to connect with this force. We make the connection by feeling freely with our open hearts.

Our permission to ourselves to make this connection is just a reflection of our love for ourselves. Every time we look in the mirror, we are giving ourselves permission to strengthen this connection.

Remember that all of life is truly an experience of you with you. Do you love yourself? Do you trust yourself? When the answer is yes to both questions, you will truly appreciate the power and magnificence that you are.

❧ ❧ ❧

Question: You spoke of a "misguided loyalty" to those who taught us all the reasons not to love ourselves. I'm a parent now, and I once was a child. I'd like to better understand this issue of loyalty. Can you say more about this?

Answer: Those of us who are parents know that we love our children and want what is best for them, even though our words and actions occasionally seem anything but loving. And as children, we may have sometimes acted in unloving ways toward our parents, usually mirroring and repeating their way of treating us.

Our loyalty to what our parents taught us and our repetition of the behaviors we copied from them is just an inexact way of expressing our love for them. When we close ourselves to feeling love for them at a deep level, we keep our connection with them alive by following their teachings at the demonstration level.

So our feeling of loyalty to parents acts as a temporary bridge until we are ready to connect with them at the level of Oneness, where the connection truly resides.

The many beliefs that our parents taught us and that we hold on to as a way of maintaining our relationship with them often plays itself out as a dance between love and hate, which reflects the dance in our own consciousness between feeling our Oneness and believing in our separation. We continue this dance in its infinite variations while our feeling of Oneness slowly and steadily intrudes into our conscious awareness.

We can support this process at any time by consciously connecting with this feeling of Oneness through the Feeling Exercise. Our feeling of Oneness is in our hearts. As we increase our feeling of love for ourselves, the love expands into a feeling of Oneness.

With the expansion of this feeling of Oneness, we come to know that we are much more than physical bodies. We begin to feel ourselves as pure consciousness, essence, which is connected to all consciousness, all essence. And we know that the unique expression of each of our essences gives vitality to all essences.

Our most precious loyalty is to the full and free expression of our true selves. Honoring our loyalty to parents and other caretakers is just one of the steps along the path to this flowering of our true selves and the deep sense of fulfillment that accompanies this unfoldment.

28

COMFORT AND DISCOMFORT, PAIN AND ECSTASY

We can always know just how much love we are feeling or withholding from ourselves by the degree of comfort or discomfort we are feeling. A sense of peace and comfort is evidence of our feeling love for ourselves. Discomfort is evidence of our withholding love. These signals, which can occur in both the physical and emotional realms, can range from excruciating pain to blissful ecstasy.

I define pain as the manifestation of fear in the physical body. And I define fear as the withholding of love, often from others and always from ourselves. At the other end of the continuum is ecstasy, an outpouring of love for ourselves and everything and everyone in the Universe.

What makes the principle around comfort and discomfort most interesting is that we are always dealing only with our perceptions. That is, it is our interpretation of a situation, rather than anything inherent in the situation, that determines whether it will be a source of comfort or discomfort to us.

To better understand this principle, we have to be willing to expand our concept of ourselves. We are not just our physical bodies. Nor are we our thoughts, beliefs, experiences, or any of the things we own or use. We are first and foremost our essence, Infinite Intelligence, God, and so is everyone and everything else. We are each the Oneness, which means that we are not separate from anyone or anything. Our discomfort arises from our misperception that we are separate from other people and things, and from God, and that we are limited to our bodies, thoughts and beliefs.

Our life in the human experience is an opportunity to transcend this misperception. We do this by learning to feel love first for ourselves and then for everyone and everything else, and by accepting everything as perfect just the way it is.

When we *feel* and know that we are primarily our essence, we will have made a great leap beyond our beliefs in the world of illusion. The process begins as we recognize that whatever thoughts, beliefs or agreements are current in the world at any time are perfect just the way they are. These thoughts, beliefs and agreements do influence how people act and the results they achieve, but they do not alter the underlying perfection that is the essence of each person and the inherent state of the Universe.

To use the signals of comfort and discomfort to their greatest advantage, we have to be willing to deal with them differently from the way we were taught. While some of us learned to run from our feelings of discomfort and pain—through drugs, alcohol, sex, work or a hundred other escape routes—others of us learned to tolerate pain, believing that such discomfort was necessary to achieve success in career, marriage, child raising and building a secure future.

Overcoming the years of intense training and the habit patterns of a lifetime is a challenge of the first order. We have to call upon all the support available to us to learn a new way to deal with the signals of pain and discomfort. When we are willing and ready to commit to doing the Feeling Exercise regularly and consistently, we will signal ourselves that we are up to that challenge.

One suggestion: When you are ready to commit to feeling your feelings, no matter how intense they may seem, and to feeling love for yourself, it is vital to provide yourself with as supportive an environment as possible—preferably a support group of one or more people who will give you unconditional love and support during this process (see Section Seven).

Remember, the Universe is a mutual support system, and each of us has a deep inner need to function in a mutually supportive environment. Providing ourselves with this environment is the path to a successful transition and ultimately to a life of total joy.

❧ ❧ ❧

Question: I have a hard time accepting that I create the pain I feel. Can you offer some support around this issue?

Answer: As challenging as it may be for you to accept, pain is a choice, an expression of your free will. Why would any of us *choose* to feel pain? Simply because the choice to feel pain validates our perception that our physical bodies are real. Every time we feel pain, we confirm to ourselves that our bodies are real.

Let's face it: We are attached to our bodies. There is nothing wrong with this choice. But the choice has consequences, and one of the consequences is pain.

The choice to favor our physicality is understandable. We have been taught that we can increase our enjoyment of life through the vehicle of our physical bodies. We can eat delicious foods, engage in sports, smell flowers, view rainbows and sunsets, and reach sexual climax. We can also run businesses, conduct scientific experiments, and make and spend money.

What we are ready to discover is that every experience we have in the physical we can enjoy beyond the physical. And what is even more significant is that we can enjoy this beyond-the-physical experience much more deeply.

Joy is a feeling. And feeling is a vibration. The higher we vibrate, the more joy we feel. The joy that we feel when we engage in a physical activity has nothing to do with the activity. Our physicality is a powerless creation of our consciousness. Our physical presence serves us best when we just allow it to be present and not make-believe it has the power to cause anything.

Pain is an illusion, a hypnotic spell we cast on ourselves when we treat our beliefs as real. We have all witnessed the acceptance of illusions as real by people under hypnosis. Tables and chairs become burning hot stoves; erasers and pencils become sharp needles.

Every belief has an illusory impact. One of our greatest illusions is the belief that our physical presence, which is really just an energy vibration, has substance. And our perception that the illusion of our physical presence can cause us pain is an even greater misperception.

Our essence is pure consciousness, and it vibrates at a high level because essence is unfettered by beliefs. When we surrender to this true state of our being, we feel the joy, the ecstasy, of this high rate of vibration. We can create, in consciousness, any experience we wish. We can eat a hamburger with raw onions and relish. We can sail on a lake, ski down a mountain or swim in the sea.

Our essence, pure consciousness, is One with all. We are free to access anything we wish in consciousness, free of calories, free of charge and free of pain.

So now I have a question for you: Do you love yourself enough to gift yourself unlimited joy? Your essence is ready when you are.

29

THE PAST AND
FORGIVENESS

Many people are drawn to focus on the past, and particularly on those parts of the past that bring up feelings of discomfort. The intention seems to be to release those parts of the past that we believe are causing us discomfort.

In reality, any part of our past that draws our attention in the present moment is part of the present. And since only the present really exists, we can only deal with our discomfort in the present.

As discussed in the previous chapter, discomfort is a signal that we are withholding love. Very often, the withholding started years earlier when we interpreted the actions of someone as unloving or unsupportive of us. Remember that for whatever reason we judge or judged someone, the result is a locking of energy, which we experience as discomfort.

Since energy, love, is constantly expanding, we must use increasing effort to repress our love. Unless we are able to release this repressed energy, we are likely to experience increasing pain and eventually disease.

How do we free the energy in judgments we might have made decades ago? The answer is by practicing forgiveness. Forgiveness is the willingness to open the energy locked up in our judgments.

As we practice feeling forgiveness for a person whom we previously judged, or are now judging, as being unloving toward us, we loosen the attachment of the judgment to the feeling. Since some of our judgments run deep and strong, it is often necessary to practice feeling forgiveness repeatedly over an extended period in order to release the judgment totally. Time is not the issue here; our willingness to forgive is what is significant.

And we are not alone in this process. The Universe is always helping us to clear all blocks to our natural state of joyfulness. It keeps offering us opportunities to forgive.

Any time we are in the presence of someone who brings up feelings of discomfort in us, we can be certain that the person is someone, *or represents someone*, whom we have not forgiven. For example, you may recall a time when you met someone at a gathering, and you had an immediate dislike for the person, even though the person did not say or do anything offensive. On an unconscious level, this person was reminding you of someone from whom you were still withholding love.

In a more personal and enduring way, our closest friends, partners, employers and associates support us in coming to peace with our past by taking on the roles of family members and other authority figures from our childhood whom we are ready to forgive.

The marvelous feature of the process is that you don't have to know whom the person represents. You merely practice forgiveness in the present moment. When you feel forgiveness for the person in your present experience, you are also forgiving whomever the person represents.

To take the matter full circle, the person you are really forgiving is yourself. When you release your judgments of another, you are in fact releasing your judgments of yourself. Your willingness to practice forgiveness for all those whom you perceived as being unloving toward you truly is a gift of self-love.

The following exercise can assist you in feeling forgiveness, and ultimately deep love, for anyone you are ready and willing to forgive. Take your time with each step. Be willing to go through the process as often as necessary until you feel deep love for the person.

The Forgiveness Exercise

For this exercise, you will want to call on the support of your Inner Self.

1. Begin by going through the three steps of the Feeling Exercise.
2. When you feel a sense of peacefulness, self-love and support, bring into your conscious awareness a person for whom you hold strong judgments.
3. Ask your Inner Self to assist you in feeling the feelings that are connected to these judgments. Feel the feelings as deeply as you can.

4. Ask your Inner Self to assist you in feeling love for these feelings. Allow your heart to open and embrace these feelings.

5. Feel deep love for your Inner Self.

6. Ask your Inner Self to assist you in feeling forgiveness for this person. Allow your heart to open as wide as you can.

7. Let this feeling of forgiveness expand into deep love for this person. When you are ready, embrace the person in this deeply felt, open-hearted love.

8. Feel your connection to the Oneness that you are.

When you are able to feel deep love for a person you previously judged, the sense of elation that comes from freeing energy that has been repressed for years can be intense. You can enjoy this kind of intensity whenever you are willing to open your heart and forgive.

❧   ❧   ❧

Question: When I think of all the people in my life whose behavior bothers me, I'm overwhelmed by the enormity of the task of forgiving them. Do you have any suggestions on how to deal with this?

Answer: How successful you will be will depend, in part, on whether you see the forgiveness process as an impossible task or a fascinating challenge. In order to master the game of life, you have to keep asking yourself, "What is the real game?" If the answer is making lots of money, having countless assets, and achieving status or fame, then the focus on the physical will take priority over honoring essence, and forgiving others will seem like an inconsequential ordeal. If you see as your purpose in life the expansion of love, joy and truth, then learning to feel forgiveness and eventually love for everyone takes on great meaning and is fun.

As greater numbers of people choose to play the real game, there is increasing support to free all the repressed energy in our many judgments and beliefs in right and wrong, good and bad. And each time more energy is freed up by one person who is willing to forgive, we all feel the expansion of love and joy.

30

━━━ ■ ━━━

HARMONY IN
RELATIONSHIPS

Every relationship in our lives reflects our relationship with ourselves. When we truly love ourselves, we attract loving, harmonious relationships with others.

What does harmony in relationships look like? The Universe provides us with the perfect model. Since the Universe is a mutual support system, the key to harmonious relationships is the willingness to support others and to allow them to support us. And how is this best accomplished? By connecting with others essence to essence and recognizing both their essence and our essence as perfect.

Anything less than perfection isn't real. It is an illusion. Anger, confusion, anxiety and fear are illusions. When we choose to interpret the behavior of ourselves or another as angry or unloving, we are just giving validity to an illusion. We are also reinforcing the belief that the illusion being presented is real. When we are willing to keep our focus on our perfect essence, both we and the other person are free to be the joyful, loving beings that we truly are.

The more we practice, the easier it becomes. A simple way to practice is to glance at each stranger as she walks toward us on the sidewalk, notice her facial expression, and then immediately go behind that expression and see her as perfect and joyful. As we increase our willingness to do this—first with strangers and then with intimate friends—we receive a fabulous benefit: We improve our ability to see ourselves as perfect and joyful.

We Always Attract to Us the People and Relationships We Want to Attract

To understand the law of attraction, let's go back to the concept of energy. Each of us emits energy signals all the time. These energy signals attract to us the precise people and relationships we want to bring into our lives in the present moment, although the choice is often on an unconscious level.

When we attract a person who acts less than lovingly toward us, that person is showing us a part of ourselves that we do not love and accept. Our Inner Self is giving us the opportunity to reconnect to a part of us from which we are withholding love. Only by our willingness to reconnect to this part of ourselves and to love it just the way it is can we open the energy that has been locked in our bodies, causing us pain and holding our power hostage.

Stated another way, everyone we attract into our lives is there to support us in reclaiming our power. When we recognize the truth of this statement, we can feel grateful for every person we encounter, every relationship we attract.

The more of our power we are willing to reclaim, the more love and trust we will feel for ourselves. The harmony we feel within will then be mirrored in the harmonious relationships we attract.

❧   ❧   ❧

Question: I have a strong sense that what you are saying is true, but I don't think my partner will go along with these ideas. What happens when one person in a close relationship chooses to play "the real game," as you call it, but the other person insists on being competitive and judgmental?

Answer: Every relationship reflects for us our own thoughts, beliefs and feelings. In a close personal relationship, such as a marriage, the reflection of thoughts and feelings can be so intense that we tend to react rather than heighten our awareness to what is really going on. In short, we become upset by the thoughts and feelings our spouses mirror for us.

Furthermore, in a marriage, there is a mutual commitment, rarely spoken of, to hold these beliefs and feelings for our spouses until our spouses are ready to accept the truth. Despite how it often appears, to those in the marriage as well as to friends and relatives, neither partner in a marriage is being unfriendly or mean. Both partners are being deeply loving and supportive of each other in learning who they really are.

Therefore, instead of seeing your partner as being unsupportive, realize that he is being very supportive. Realize, too, that your best support of him is to love and accept him just the way he is, for in truth, he is precisely the way he is in order to support you.

His competitive and judgmental behavior is reflecting the part of you that is still attached to competition and judgment. As you are able to love and accept him as he is, you make peace with the part of yourself that he is reflecting. As your love for him and for yourself deepens, his need to maintain his competitive, judgmental behavior will almost certainly diminish.

Our partners are our perfect and persistent mirrors for us. When we are willing to value them and acknowledge their dedicated support of us, we make one of the best investments in our mutual growth that we can make.

31

THE UNIVERSE
HANDLES THE DETAILS

Taking care of the details of our lives generally is considered a rational-mind activity. We assume that the best way, the only way, to make decisions and plan events is to use our thinking minds to figure things out.

However, our thinking minds do not know all the variables of any situation. Only our Infinite Intelligence has this greater knowledge. As we learn to relinquish our rational thinking and let our intuition— our connection to Infinite Intelligence—guide the way, we discover how easily and effortlessly events unfold for us.

I'm sure we can each recall numerous situations where seemingly chance encounters led to valuable outcomes beyond anything we could ever have planned. An example from my own experience occurred in 1982, not long after I had started leading workshops. One evening, at a preview of a workshop being held in a New York apartment, a woman attended whom I did not know, and she left before we were introduced. Six months later, she called to ask me to lead a workshop. The woman, Patricia Horan, was a writer and contributing editor for *New Realities* magazine. Shortly thereafter, the publisher of the magazine, James Bolen, decided to do a cover story on me. He has since become a dear and trusted friend, and a great support in my second career.

At no time during this remarkable series of events did I try to reach the outcome that ensued. The Universe, in Its infinite wisdom, handled every detail perfectly.

Letting our intuition lead the way does not mean we resign from active participation in life. Quite the contrary. When we allow our Infinite Intelligence to guide us, we may be inspired to express ourselves in ways we never would have imagined. And as we develop trust in the process, we act with certainty and feel the confidence of receiving benefit from whatever events occur.

Following our inner guidance always increases the flow of energy in and around us, and makes participation in life more interesting and fun. It also yields the most creative outcomes—for everyone involved.

One point I wish to stress: The statement that the Universe handles the details does not mean that the Universe handles the details we assign to It. When our rational minds take control, we are on our own; we have to handle our own details. Only by surrendering to our Infinite Intelligence can we trust that the Universe will handle the details in ways that are truly supportive of us and everyone else.

There is one other aspect of this principle that is helpful to recognize. When we each express our talents freely, all the tasks necessary to support our free expression are handled efficiently and smoothly. Moreover, the products and services that come out of this pure expression of love are of the highest quality.

When we express from our essence, the Universe supports us at the deepest level. We are then free to share our talents with confidence, joy and true creative energy.

❧   ❧   ❧

Question: Are you saying that planning is a waste of time?

Answer: Yes. Planning is a function of our thinking minds, and when our thinking minds are active, we shut out our Infinite Intelligence, which is capable of guiding our lives perfectly every moment.

Our beliefs that life is a struggle and that we have to figure things out may be entrenched, but that does not make them true. The truth is that the Universe gives us signals every moment, and as we learn to listen to and follow these signals, we find that things fall into place in what often seem miraculous ways. We don't have to plan at all.

This is a radical departure from the way we were taught. It's important to realize that, from our limited vantage point in the world of illusion, we can see only certain variables, options or possibilities from which to choose. From the much more expansive vantage point of Infinite Intelligence, all variables are known.

We all have felt the joy and freedom that comes from spontaneous occurrences. The traditional approach of our society is to squelch all opportunities for spontaneity. Learning to trust in the loving support of our Universe can take time, but the benefits are well worth it, for we can enjoy not only the Universe handling the details, but the spontaneity that comes from developing trust in the Universe.

There are times when it is appropriate to make future arrangements. At these times, we check in with our intuition to discover the most supportive course of action. Our intuition in the present guides us in acting in the future.

Question: If we aren't meant to plan, can you suggest what we can do to prepare for the day?

Answer: I recommend starting the day with the Feeling Exercise, ideally in front of a mirror. Remember, our feelings connect us to our intuition, which is our access point to Infinite Intelligence. As we learn to pay more attention to our feelings and to the energy within them, and less attention to our thoughts, we will develop our capacity to listen to and follow the signals our Infinite Intelligence is always sending us. These signals are the guideposts for our lives.

There is really only one way to learn to trust your intuition. Try it! Focus on your feelings, pay attention to any insights that come to you, follow (or don't follow) your intuitive signals, and notice the results. And enjoy the process.

ক্ট   ক্ট   ক্ট

My intuition tells me we're ready for a break.

SECTION SIX

MEANS AND ENDS

32

MEANS AND ENDS
ARE THE SAME

We are a society dedicated to end results, to goals, and many of us spend a great portion of our lives working to achieve goals. Some of these goals are set by other people, most often by our parents or other authority figures. Other goals we set for ourselves.

The high achievers among us are relentless in fulfilling their goals, and there is much respect for and many rewards offered to these high achievers. Moreover, as a society, we hold the belief that the ends justify the means. The person who risks his health, happiness, family and friends to fulfill his goals is considered a model of success.

To a remarkable degree, we are willing and ready to sacrifice the present moment for some future goal. One of the most common examples of this phenomenon is the person who works hard at a job for forty years—a job that is not fulfilling—in order to retire with a pension so that he may enjoy a life of ease and contentment.

We wage wars as a way to assure peace. We punish people thinking that punishment will reduce crime. We believe that we can achieve a certain result by taking an opposite action. And although we have mounds of evidence to the contrary, we continue to hold on to the belief that the ends justify the means.

The truth is simple and direct: Means and ends are the same. The means chosen to achieve a result become the result.

- To achieve peace, we feel and express our inner peacefulness, moment by moment.
- To experience unconditional love and support, we feel and express our unconditional love and support for everyone and everything in every moment.
- To enjoy a life that works perfectly, we see and feel the perfection of everything and everyone, including ourselves, at all times.
- To experience the natural abundance of the Universe, we feel and express gratitude for the abundance all around us.

The principle is profoundly simple. How we choose to express ourselves results in the outcome we attain.

❦ ❦ ❦

Question: You make it sound so simple and easy—as if all we have to do to have our lives work perfectly is to feel loving and joyful. Are you really saying we don't have to *do* anything to be happy and successful?

Answer: We are *beings*, not *doings*. However, we are taught the opposite, and thus we spend our lives "doing" as a way of justifying our beliefs that life is a struggle, that everything we receive must be earned by working for it, that people are competitive and adversarial by nature, and that an open heart is an invitation to be hurt. As long as we hold on to these beliefs, we have to constantly *do* things to substantiate them.

When each of us is naturally expressing from our open hearts, all that needs to be provided comes forth with ease and joy. This is one of the ways we experience the inherent abundance of the Universe.

We can "do" the laundry or the dishes as a task, or we can express our gratitude for the clothes, the dishes, the water and soap, the washer and dryer—all of which we generally take for granted. When our focus is on being grateful, we enjoy folding clothes or putting our hands in warm, soapy water.

No matter how hard we each work at being a *doing*, we will always be a *being*. Why not accept being who we really are? Then we can put bumper stickers on our cars that say, "Being is more fun!"

33

———————————————

HOW TO ACCEPT THE RESULTS WE ARE CREATING

We know that our thinking minds are capable of creating or attracting circumstances that cause us discomfort. Yet there is a great temptation to put the blame on other people or on the circumstances, even though we know that placing control of our lives outside of us is disempowering.

In order to keep our power within us or to reclaim any that we have already vested in people or circumstances outside of us, it is important to remind ourselves that we have created whatever is in our lives. We also want to remind ourselves that this creation is always purposeful.

Next, we make peace with the situation just the way it is. To do this, we often need to acknowledge that no situation or person is bad or good, right or wrong. Learning to release our judgments takes patience and perseverance.

YOU CAN HAVE IT ALL

Only through coming to peace with the situation can we open our hearts and feel that we are valuable and essential parts of a larger experience that binds each of us to everyone else—a large mutual support system comprising many smaller support systems.

Our basic instinct is to live in harmony with everyone and everything. As we practice being loving and supportive of ourselves and others in the face of all the dramatic circumstances we keep seeing, we shall gradually reduce the number of dramatic incidents and begin creating an environment that is loving, supportive, nurturing and harmonious. In fact, the process is already underway.

❧ ❧ ❧

Question: I don't have a problem with blaming other people as much as I do with blaming myself. I find I get very angry with myself when my life isn't working. Can you offer any suggestions?

Answer: Yes. Let me begin by saying that you are sitting on a gold mine of energy without realizing it. That energy, remember, is love. Anger or any other so-called negative emotion is just love repressed by a judgment of it as being something other than love.

Furthermore, the perception that there is a difference between being angry at another person and being angry at yourself is an illusion. We are all One; there is no separation.

We each have only two choices when it comes to love. We can allow love to flow freely and enjoy it, or we can repress it and create discomfort. Our judgments and labels of our feelings just lock in energy (love). Whenever we repress energy, which is the source of our power, we feel that power diminish and our vulnerability grow.

My suggestion to you is to focus on increasing your feelings of love for yourself. The huge amount of love that is bottled up by your anger is just waiting to be reclaimed. As you open your heart to yourself, your sense of personal power will grow and your sense of vulnerability will diminish. In addition, whenever you begin the process of feeling love for yourself, you will notice a sense of ease replacing the effort you expended to repress the energy (love) that was crying out to be released.

I also suggest that you acknowledge, in this moment and every moment, that you are your own best friend. If you get angry at your best friend, how do you resolve the conflict? You remind yourself how precious a best friend is, you let go of your judgments, and you shower your best friend with love.

34

OWNING THE LEVEL

O nce we have achieved mastery of anything in our lives, we own the level attained by that achievement. Furthermore, the skills acquired to attain that level are transferable. We see illustrations of this principle all the time.

Look at the business section of your newspaper and you will often see that a president of a major corporation has transferred to another major corporation whose product or service is totally different from the product or service of the company that he left. Once a person functions at a presidential level, he owns that level and moves around in society at that level.

In our society, we use a hierarchical system to rate various skills and talents. A person who is talented in business or in a profession is usually accorded a higher status than one whose talent is sewing, cooking, repairing appliances or hanging wallpaper. Furthermore, this situation is likely to remain in place as long as the people involved accept the existing standard.

In truth, every talent is equal in value to every other talent. For those who have a skill or talent that is not usually accorded high status and value, it is important to recognize this truth, because far more important than the value placed on a skill or talent by society is the value placed on it by the individual who has the skill.

When our perception of the value of our talent increases, so will the actual value of it to others. The person who prepares food, lays tiles or raises children with great skill is entitled to the same acknowledgment as is the successful president of a major corporation. Each of us is entitled to be treated as a superstar in our area of expertise. However, until we view ourselves and our talents as valuable, no one else will.

The main issue we are dealing with is self-love. All the reasons we have for not loving ourselves act as obstacles to our expressing our talents in ways that are self-supportive and fulfilling.

One of the most significant ways we withhold love from ourselves is our resistance to making peace with the past. Until we come to peace with all of our childhood relationships, particularly those with parents and other caretakers, we are apt to block the full expression of our talents.

If, after we feel deep love for ourselves and our parents, we are still not able to express our talents in self-supportive and fulfilling ways, we are probably still attached to struggle or some other similar belief.

In our area of talent, we are all potential superstars. Since along with every talent come the tools to express it perfectly, we can become superstars whenever we are ready. And others will view us as superstars when we view ourselves that way.

❧ ❧ ❧

Question: Are you saying that once we have achieved some success at any one thing, the skills and consciousness developed to attain that success are transferable?

Answer: That is exactly what I am saying. In practical terms, this means that when our career focus and talents merge, we can enjoy a level of success that is equivalent to the greatest success we have ever achieved. In fact, as we deepen our love for ourselves, we are likely to reach a much higher level. The energy of self-love is so powerful and creative that it can remarkably improve the quality of our lives.

Question: I enjoy expressing my artistic talent through the medium of clay. My pieces are of excellent quality, and I receive constant acknowledgment for the beauty of my work. I would like to leave my job and support myself through my artistic expression, but I'm not sure that I'm ready. Can you comment on this?

Answer: There are several issues here to be aware of. First, I suggest you keep your present source of income to allow you to feel comfortable financially. Express your artistic talent in your free time.

Next, look at your present life. How effective are you in dealing with money? In other words, what level of financial success do you own? If you are comfortable with money and it moves easily in your life right now, then you can expect this to continue as you move into your new career.

On the other hand, if you have issues around money, you can be sure those issues will continue to have an impact until you expand your consciousness. Remember, we always experience in the physical world an exact outplaying of the state of our consciousness. If your present situation with money is less than comfortable, take the time to increase your feelings of self-love and to make peace with all of your relationships, including your relationship with money.

Look closely at your beliefs about money. Many people have receiving money and working hard tied together. In other words, they hold the belief that money comes in only if it is *earned* in some way. Allowing money and other aspects of abundance simply to be present in our lives, for no other reason than that it is the natural order, calls for great intention.

If your present situation with money is less than comfortable, open the energy repressed by your beliefs about money by going through the Feeling Exercise. And be patient. Take small steps and celebrate each successful step you take. Use your support group to reflect and expand your love for yourself.

Also, remember that Infinite Intelligence is on your side, ready to support you whenever you are willing to open to Its love and guidance.

35

———■———

THE SPONGE

Our consciousness is like a sponge. It absorbs whatever is in its immediate environment.

In our society there are powerful influences surrounding each of us all the time—television, radio, newspapers, magazines, films, videos, salespeople, employers, relatives and friends. These media and people have many ideas about what we should be thinking and doing. When we avoid making clear choices about the quality of life we wish, we tend to adopt the ideas put forth by these other sources, often without being aware that we are doing so.

To offset this tendency, we can choose to hold a clear intention to feel self-loving, peaceful and joyful despite what circumstances arise. We can choose to do the Feeling Exercise whenever we are in discomfort. We can keep the quality of life we wish for ourselves uppermost in our consciousness. The choice is always ours. When we avoid making this choice, others make it for us.

Fill your own sponge with the intention to see the perfection in everything just the way it is and to stay connected to the peaceful, joyful energy of your essence.

❧   ❧   ❧

Question: I know people who refuse to read newspapers or watch television because they don't want to be influenced by the negativity in these media. Would you recommend that we all stop reading newspapers and listening to the news?

Answer: First of all, there is no such thing as negativity. We interpret something as negative or bad only because it triggers some judgment that we are still holding on to. I personally use newspapers and television as a way to bring any judgments I have to my conscious awareness. I can then use the Feeling Exercise to reclaim the power I have vested in the people and circumstances that I have judged.

Another way I use the media is to evoke feelings of compassion for all the people who are reaching out for love and support. When I feel compassion for these people, the love I feel for myself and for everyone else also increases.

Our willingness to go beyond outer appearances and to connect our essence with the essence of all those who are sharing the planet with us is empowering for us and for those whose essence we touch. We are all connected and our gift of love is always appreciated, even though the gift may be received without the recipients' conscious awareness.

36

SAFETY

There is total safety in the Universe at all times. We feel that safety when we are giving unconditional love and support to others or when we are receiving unconditional love and support. Put another way, we feel safe when we are in touch with our own essence and with the essence of all others.

We do not have to do anything to save ourselves or the Universe. Furthermore, acting out of a sense of urgency only creates more urgency. When we feel the peace of the Universe, we can express fully and freely who we really are in ways that truly support everyone.

Our essence, and the essence of everything in the Universe, is eternal. Until we fully accept this truth, we will live in continual fear that something bad, terrible or painful can happen to us at any time.

Since our essence cannot experience pain or death, we are free to express who we really are and to live a life of joy forever. We can begin whenever we are ready.

ℛ   ℛ   ℛ

Question: Your statement that we don't have to do anything to save ourselves or the Universe brings to mind the environmental groups and the human and animal rights groups. Can you say more about the idea that we don't have to save anyone or anything?

Answer: The groups that you refer to are motivated by the love they feel for the environment, other humans and animals. The support they offer is most effective when the activities they engage in are expressions of the love they feel.

There are times when some of the individuals in these groups see those who are not kind and supportive of other humans, animals and the environment as "bad guys" who must be stopped. In most cases, their intention is honorable, but they miss an important point. Remember that whenever we judge others, we lock the energy around the very circumstances we are unhappy with and achieve the exact opposite of the result we would like.

The solution is always to release our judgments, to free the energy—the love—repressed by our judgments, and to send that love, essence to essence, to the person or persons from whom we were withholding love. In other words, we bypass the circumstances altogether and instead feel love for the essence of those involved in the circumstances.

Environmental and human degradation is an illusion that we have all bought into and one that we will not be able to see beyond until we surrender the beliefs that create this illusion and trust that our essence is real. Free of the belief in toxicity, for example, we are able to align our loving essence in harmony with everything.

Love is the only true healing force in the Universe. Our willingness to feel love for everyone under all circumstances can create miracles, which we are beginning to see more frequently around the world.

37

QUIET, HARMONY
AND RHYTHM

There is a basic rhythm to the Universe, and each of us has a rhythm that is in natural harmony with this universal rhythm. There is a rhythm to our walk, to our speech, to our eating, to our playing golf and tennis. There is a rhythm to our relating to others. Life is so sweet when we hear, feel and follow these rhythms. But we have to be quiet to hear and feel them.

The Infinite Intelligence of the Universe is behind these rhythms. As we become more sensitive to them, we pick up the natural guidance that is there for us at all times.

The world of illusion, with its customary disregard for what is natural, simple and easy, creates so much background noise that often we cannot hear and feel these rhythms. We can choose to create more quiet in our lives in order to hear and feel these basic rhythms. Our increased sensitivity will bring to us even more peaceful environments in which to enjoy our lives. As a result, we will have a deeper appreciation for the magnificent harmony that is always present in the Universe.

Meditation

One of the best ways to learn to distinguish between what is real and what is an illusion is through the practice of meditation. This is quiet time devoted to connecting to our real selves and to the Infinite Intelligence of the Universe. This is also a time to feel our connection to the essence of all others.

Meditation leads us to a state of peacefulness. It is only in a state of peacefulness that we can be truly creative and fully and freely express who we really are. We feel peaceful when we know that whatever is perfect for us is a gift from the Universe, awaiting our readiness to receive it.

Meditation also provides an opportunity to be in touch with the life force behind the infinite supply of energy in the Universe, that which connects and supports all of us—love. Fear, anxiety or any other emotional state is simply the result of our withholding love from ourselves and others. When we meditate, the peacefulness we feel opens us to the love of the Universe, which we can then allow to flow through us and through everything and everyone else.

38

UNCOVERING JOY

J oy is part of our essence, the underlying feeling that we all have access to. We each have a basic love of joy and a deep desire to relate to one another in joyful ways.

However, most of us have buried our joy beneath layers of judgments and repressed feelings. The challenge before us is to keep peeling off the layers until the joy is uncovered and allowed to fill and overflow from our being.

There is no substitute for this procedure, and it is a truly personal journey for each of us. We cannot do it for another. We can only support a person who is going through the process himself.

The principles discussed in this book are the intellectual justification for accepting that our joy is real. We will know the truth of these principles only when we open our hearts and allow ourselves to feel their validity. Connecting with the principles at the feeling level inspires us to release the joy within and to allow it to become an ever-increasing part of our lives.

Of one thing we can be certain: Joy will always be there—in us and in everyone else. The quality of our lives thus depends upon:

1. the degree to which we are willing to recognize that the feeling of joy is real;
2. the degree to which we are willing to release the joy within; and
3. the degree to which we recognize that the only obstacle to releasing joy is our unwillingness to open our hearts and feel love for ourselves, and through our open hearts to feel love for everyone and everything.

A good way to practice feeling joy is to do the Feeling Exercise consistently. The more we connect with the joy within, the more real it becomes for us.

Put another way, if we wish to achieve a life of total joy, we have to be willing to connect with the joy that is our essence. Remember: Means and ends are the same. To achieve joy, we feel and express the joy within us every moment.

❧   ❧   ❧

Let's take another break. Then we'll look at one of the most effective means for integrating Universal Principles into our lives—the mutual support group.

SECTION SEVEN

THE SUPPORT GROUP

39

THE VALUE OF THE
MUTUAL SUPPORT GROUP

As human beings, our most basic desire is to love and be loved unconditionally. Our natural inclination is to mutually support one another.

However, given our years of training in the competitive-adversarial model, we have learned to close our hearts and shut off our feelings, both to ourselves and others. Our beliefs in separation, scarcity and struggle have led us to fear and compete against each other. The result has been increasing pain and a growing sense of powerlessness, not only individually but as a society.

Many of us are now ready and eager to reconnect to our true selves—the powerful beings that we really are—and to assist others in doing the same. In reconnecting to who we are, we connect to our Oneness, which is the source of our power.

The value of the mutual support group is that it provides a safe and nurturing environment in which to practice giving and receiving unconditional love and support, reconnecting with our feelings, and reclaiming our power. In such an environment, we learn to express qualities that lead to truly fulfilling lives: honesty, trust, surrender, compassion, generosity, humor, playfulness, creativity, openness, integrity.

There is now in existence a growing network of no-cost mutual support groups that meet weekly in towns and cities in North and Central America, western Europe, Australia and the Middle East. Some of these groups have been meeting for nearly a decade; others are newly formed. Each one shares a commitment to give and receive support in living by Universal Principles.

The following material can assist you in starting a mutual support group of your own. It takes only two willing people to start a group and the intention and self-love to stay with the process.

40

—————

SUGGESTED GUIDELINES FOR SUPPORT GROUP MEETINGS

B e sure to go over the following guidelines with everyone who wants to be part of a support group, and review the guidelines periodically. If there are any guidelines your group wishes to modify, I suggest you take the matter up before a meeting rather than during a meeting.

1. Be clear about the intention for the support group: to create an environment in which to practice unconditional love and mutual support; to assist each other in connecting to our feelings and reclaiming our power; and to expand our level of trust in ourselves, in each other, and in the power of our Oneness.

2. Make the commitment to refrain from discussions and advice-giving during the meeting. This is a most significant guideline and one that is often disregarded. Remember that

we best support others in their personal empowerment by letting them deal with their unique challenges and discover their own solutions.

3. Agree on a starting time and length of meeting (usually 1½ to 2 hours) and honor the agreement.

4. Rotate the meeting site, unless the meeting is held at a public facility, such as a business or community center.

5. Notify someone if you will be late or absent from a meeting.

6. Rotate facilitators.

7. Agree to follow the Support Group Format until all participants are fully familiar with the exercises. Thereafter, adaptations may be made by mutual agreement of the group.

8. Honor the confidentiality of personal matters brought up during meetings.

9. Be clear about participant and guest policies, and take time before meetings to inform new participants and guests about the group guidelines.

10. Support the purpose of the group by gently and lovingly reminding participants when the guidelines are not being observed.

41

GROUP PURPOSE

Whenever two or more people choose to join together as a group, one of the first and most essential exercises the members can take part in is to define their group purpose. In the same way that a person's individual purpose creates the inspiration for her life, the group purpose creates the inspiration for the life of the group.

Prior to defining the group purpose, however, it is important for each participant to first feel the inspiration of his individual purpose. The energy that flows from this inspiration serves as the foundation for the creation of the group purpose.

The group purpose, then, is the second part of a two-part process. Without the first part in place, the second part is unsupported. Therefore, only when the individual purposes are in place is the group ready to define its group purpose.

To arrive at the group purpose, I suggest that the participants join in a short meditation and allow a feeling to emerge from a place of peacefulness and connection. Each participant then chooses one word that expresses this feeling: *love, joy, peace, commitment, power, harmony, trust, fun, Oneness,* etc. From this input, the group develops a simple statement of purpose with which everyone resonates.

Some examples of group purposes:

> ✣ *We joyfully commit to expressing peace, joy and harmony.*
> ✣ *Our purpose is expanding love and laughter.*
> ✣ *We join in divine play; we open to divine power.*

As with individual purposes, the group purpose is about the feeling quality, not about the words. Ideally, the feeling quality gives rise to the words, so that thereafter, when the words are spoken or brought into consciousness, these words reconnect the participants to the feeling of their group purpose.

While there is no urgency to arrive at a statement of group purpose at the first meeting, it is important to make this a priority item on the agenda at each meeting until everyone feels inspired and in alignment with the group purpose. The creation of a group purpose that inspires each member is key to the success of the group.

Defining our purpose in universal terms aligns us with the power of the Universe. When a group aligns with the Universe, the power expressed through the group is expanded enormously. Every member of the group not only feels this power but also enjoys the confidence and certainty that this power brings.

When new members join the group, be sure they have the opportunity to add their input to the purpose. Also, I suggest you revise the group purpose periodically so that it continues to inspire all participants.

Defining the Group Purpose
Within Existing Groups

The foregoing recommendations apply to a group that is about to form. If you are in an existing group—be it a marriage, partnership, social club, business venture or any other kind of group—and you wish to align in purpose, the approach is somewhat different.

If there is any discomfort within the group, you will first want to come to peace with your relationship with the group. Discomfort in a group means either that the group purpose has not been defined (or not been defined at a universal level) or that one or more of the participants are not aligned with that purpose. In either case, begin by going through the three steps of the Feeling Exercise until you feel love for yourself just the way you are. Remember that you cannot feel love for another until you feel love for yourself.

Next, be willing to let go of all the judgments you hold about any others in the group. These judgments lock the energy within you. If you notice any judgments, begin practicing forgiveness for all those whom you are judging. Continue the practice daily until all judgment is released. Then shift the focus to feeling unconditional love for each of the other group members. Remind yourself that whenever you judge another, you are really judging a part of yourself. When you feel unconditional love for another person, you are feeling love for a part of yourself from which you previously withheld love.

Time is not a factor. It is helpful to be patient and to allow as long as it takes to come to peace with existing relationships. Only when you come to peace with these relationships are you ready to align in purpose. At this point, you can follow the procedure for defining the group purpose outlined at the beginning of the chapter.

Every group has the potential to be a perfect support group. Even if you are the only one in the group who is willing to see the others as perfect just the way they are, that willingness on your part is sufficient to open the energy of the group in a very significant way.

Of course, it is helpful for as many participants as possible to express unconditional love and support for each other. Unconditional love and support does not mean anyone has to do anything outwardly. There is no obligation to give money or other material support, to spend time with someone, or to do anything else, although an outward action can occur. All the "doing" is at the consciousness level. When we express love and support at the level of consciousness, our love and support is reflected in our daily experiences.

The definition and redefinition of group purpose is the single most valuable activity for any group to engage in. Having an inspiring group purpose and redefining it from time to time guarantees not only success for the group, but success for the participants as well, beyond their activities in the group.

42

SUPPORT GROUP EXERCISES

The following exercises have been developed over a decade and are meant to be used at support group meetings as a way to help fulfill the intentions of the group. The exercises are explained in detail below and are outlined in the Support Group Format in Chapter 43.

The Invocation

At the beginning of each meeting, someone in the group volunteers to read the Invocation. The purpose of the Invocation is to remind participants of the support that is always available and to provide an opportunity to consciously connect with this support. It is also meant to connect participants with the Oneness of which we are all a part.

The group is free to modify the Invocation if participants wish and if everyone feels more comfortable with the modifications.

Invocation

We ask for the support of all in the Universe
who are aligned with us in consciousness,
including our Infinite Intelligence, God,
in assisting us in awakening;
in assisting us in opening our hearts,
and inspiring and empowering us to support
each other so that we may all
experience the truth about ourselves.
We ask for support in consciousness
in feeling our connection
with everyone and everything
in the Universe at all times,
so that we can truly say and feel,
"We are One."

The Power of Peace Meditation

The Peace Meditation is a beautiful gift from Grady Claire Porter.* Each statement of the meditation begins with the words "I feel." I strongly encourage the person reading the meditation as well as those listening to it to really connect to the statements at a feeling level.

The Peace Meditation

I feel, with unconditional trust, that I am the
whole of the Universe, and all that I see is Me.

---

*Author of *Conversations with JC* (High View Publishing, 1981)

I feel, at my deepest level,
the power of being who I am.

I feel the willingness and the readiness
to exercise the power of being who I am.

I feel the gentleness of my own power,
and the absolute certainty of knowing
that my power is the power of peace.

I feel the conviction and trust of my Self so totally
that I no longer need to project anything but
absolute and unconditional love.

I feel, in totality, the infinite variety
of my Beingness.

I feel the warmth and peace of unconditionally
loving my own Infinite Self.

And, at this deep feeling level, I this moment yield to the
power of my Self, totally trusting my unconditional love and
support for all of Me, and accept all that I see as the
expression and experience of this power.

The Feeling Exercise

During a support group meeting, the Feeling Exercise may be used
in various ways. The group may choose to go through the exercise
silently together. One participant may lead several others through the
exercise while the rest of the participants send loving support, after

which participants switch roles. Or if one participant is experiencing very intense feelings, he may ask to be supported by the entire group in going through the Feeling Exercise, which follows:

Close your eyes and scan your body. Notice how you are feeling. Then:

1. Feel the feeling free of any thoughts you have about it. Feel the energy, the power, in the feeling.
2. Feel love for the feeling just the way it is. Feel love for the power in the feeling.
3. Feel love for yourself feeling the feeling and feeling the power in the feeling.

Note: The word "love" has been so misused in our society that some people may have an initial aversion to the word, particularly those who experienced very abusive childhoods. Let your intuition guide you in taking someone through the exercise. You might, for example, try replacing the word "love" with "compassion" or "acceptance."

The Self-Empowerment Exercise

When someone in a support group is experiencing very intense feelings around a particular circumstance or situation and feels the need for greater support than the Feeling Exercise offers, another group member can volunteer to gently and lovingly guide the person through the following eleven-step procedure. Other group members provide additional support by listening with unconditional love.

The person who volunteers to take a participant through the exercise (it may or may not be the group facilitator) reads the following statements or questions, being sure to allow plenty of time for the participant to respond to each statement.

1. Describe the situation in as few words as you need.
2. Close your eyes and focus your awareness on how you are feeling in relationship to this situation. . . . Can you feel the feeling? Can you feel the energy, the vibration, in the feeling?
3. Are you willing to stay with the feeling and to allow it to be just the way it is?
4. Can you feel love (or compassion) for the feeling? Are you willing to receive support in feeling love for the feeling? Can you feel the support coming in?
5. Are you willing to accept the purposefulness of this situation, even if you don't understand what the purpose is at this time?
6. Are you willing to let go of your interpretation of this situation as being bad or wrong?
7. If there is someone else or others involved in the situation, can you accept that you attracted them to support you in reclaiming your power?
8. Can you see and feel the perfection of what is just the way it is?
9. Feel the essence that you truly are. Connect this loving essence with the essence of everyone involved in the situation.

10. Allow your heart to open and this feeling of love to expand. . . . When the love has expanded sufficiently, let it embrace the situation and all those involved in the situation, including yourself.

11. Feel love for yourself feeling all this love, and all the power contained in this love. . . . Feel this power as your own.

Note: If a person has difficulty with any of the steps, suggest that he or she stay with the feelings, open to support in feeling love for the feelings, and continue with the exercise at a later time.

This is an exercise in opening energy around repressed feelings. In situations where the energy has been repressed for a long time, the process may require some patience. However, just a person's willingness to go through the exercise starts the process in motion. Remember, the energy wants to be released, and there is support at all levels to release it.

The Positive-Reflection Exercise

Participants focus on one person at a time. In turn, each participant looks the recipient in the eyes and says, "The positive qualities I see in you that you reflect for me are . . ." and completes the statement with several qualities that spontaneously come up, such as *kindness, exuberance, wisdom, joyfulness*. The recipient merely says, "Thank you," and the exercise continues until everyone has had an opportunity to receive recognition from all participants.

Note: Be sure to give each recipient a few moments to take in and feel the effect of these loving words before going on to the next person.

Variations on the Positive-Reflection Exercise

If there is not enough time to do the full exercise, each participant can recognize just the person to his left, going around the circle to the right. Or the exercise may be shortened by stating just one quality per person.

Requests for Support in Consciousness

The game of life is played at the level of consciousness. Unencumbered by beliefs, our consciousness expresses our Infinite Intelligence. Asking for support in consciousness is a way of accessing this unconditionally loving part of ourselves. We frame each request in terms of Universal Principles.

For example, someone who is having difficulty paying his bills on time might make this request for support:

> I ask for support in consciousness in feeling my feelings around shortage, remembering that abundance is our natural state, and feeling gratitude for all that I have.

A person who is experiencing physical or emotional pain might make this request:

> I ask for support in consciousness in fully feeling my feelings, feeling love for my feelings, and feeling love for myself just the way I am.

Someone who is having a conflict with a member of her family or with a person at work might frame the request in this way:

> I ask for support in consciousness in feeling forgiveness for this person and for myself, and in connecting to our Oneness.

While it is helpful to ask for support in consciousness in quiet meditation alone, the impact is greater when the request is made at a support group meeting or in the presence of one or more people who are willing to offer their support. Also, the request is stronger when it is stated in the positive.

Listen carefully to yourself as you ask for support. Notice the amount of intention your request carries. If your request has less than 100 percent intention, and you really wish to have what you are asking for, then ask again at subsequent support group meetings. Continue asking until you feel that you have reached 100 percent intention and you have communicated your level of intention to the group.

Asking for support in consciousness is one of the simplest, most powerful and enjoyable ways to expand your consciousness and thus transform your life. I recommend making this practice an integral part of your daily routine.

Acknowledgments

One of the cornerstones of the support group process is the use of acknowledgments to express or to send love and support in a very direct, focused way. The words used are less important than the heart-felt intention behind the words.

After a participant has stated her purpose or asked for support in consciousness, the other participants acknowledge the person by sending loving energy to her—through their eyes, hearts and hands—as they make a mutually-agreed-upon declaration of support, such as those suggested in the Support Group Format.

43

FORMAT FOR A
SUPPORT GROUP
MEETING

1. Following brief introductions, choose a facilitator for the meeting, or allow one to emerge spontaneously.
2. Center the energy in the group: hold hands, close eyes, quiet minds, *focus awareness on feelings.*
3. Read the Invocation (page 184) and, if you wish, the Power of Peace Meditation (pages 184-85).
4. Offer participants the opportunity to go through the Feeling Exercise (pages 185-86) or the Self-Empowerment Exercise (pages 186-88).
5. State individual purposes (see Chapter 26, pages 119-21).
   Acknowledgment: "(*Name*), I love you and support you in feeling inspired by your purpose." (See page 190.)
6. State the group purpose (see Chapter 41, pages 179-80).
7. Review one or two Universal Principles.

8. Share success stories in using Universal Principles or in making previous requests for support in consciousness.

9. Take a few moments to feel and express gratitude.
   Acknowledgment: "We feel and expand our gratitude for the gifts of love we receive."

10. The Positive-Reflection Exercise (see page 188).

11. Requests for support in consciousness (see pages 189-90).
   Acknowledgment: "(*Name*), I love you and support you just the way you are in all your power and magnificence."

12. Closing: hold hands, close eyes, and allow the group energy to expand. Participants may either bring into consciousness silently or name aloud people to whom they wish to send this loving and supportive energy.

13. Set next meeting. Make announcements.

Note: The sequence of this format may be modified to support the continuity of energy within a particular support group.

SECTION EIGHT

BEYOND BASICS

44

CREATIVITY

There are two ways to express our creativity. The way most of us have chosen is with our beliefs. Whatever our thinking minds believe, our creativity brings into being. If we believe in struggle, our creativity will bring to us many different circumstances that give us the opportunity to struggle. If we believe in pain, our creativity will bring to us circumstances that cause us pain.

Since we all have many beliefs, our creativity is busily engaged in demonstrating to us the validity of these beliefs. If we pay attention to our circumstances, we have a clear view of our beliefs. Seen from this aspect, our creativity is most useful.

The other way we express our creativity is by allowing our Infinite Intelligence, our Divinity, to lead the way. This all-knowing part of us brings into being all of the joy, harmony, support, abundance and unconditional love we can handle.

This part of us creates with ease and simplicity whenever we let go of a belief. We can fairly call these creations "beyond belief," for they are just that. Creations that come from our Infinite Intelligence are both magnificent and beyond our thinking minds' capacity to understand.

What is important to keep in our awareness is that each of us is the perfect vehicle to give this extraordinary creativity the opportunity to express. Without our cooperation, these unlimited gifts of beauty, harmony, peacefulness, abundance and unconditional love do not come to pass.

We are always at choice. We chose, by agreement, to take on the beliefs we did for the purpose of opening the energy around them so that this energy could be freed to express as our divine creativity.

Behind what appears to be a tragedy is a divine comedy. There is great humor in a world filled with divine beings who have all power, who are all-knowing, who have been gifted with unlimited abundance and joyfulness and—just for good measure—eternal life, and who make believe—with great ingenuity—that they are powerless, fear-ridden, competitive and adversarial, greedy, vengeful and mortal.

In the absence of our willingness to surrender to our divine creativity, we can at least laugh at how delightfully ludicrous we are.

45

THE ILLUSION OF CHANGE

O ne of the most popular and misunderstood concepts of our time is the concept of change. Hardly a day goes by that we don't hear about the need for change, the desire for change. In support of this widespread belief, many of us change jobs, change homes, change partners—repeatedly and persistently.

One astute observer remarked, "The more things change, the more they stay the same." The author of this statement was able to discern the distinction between form and substance, and to recognize that the underlying dynamics of change always continue in full force and effect. The form may change, but the substance remains the same.

To better understand these dynamics, let's take a look at change from the standpoint of Universal Principles. The desire to change something usually signifies a dissatisfaction with a present circumstance. This means that in some way we are being judgmental; we are not at peace with the circumstance just the way it is.

The principle involved is nonjudgment, and the consequence of its violation is that whenever we judge someone or something, we immediately lock the energy tightly around the circumstance and it stays frozen the way it is. Thus, the result of being judgmental is precisely the opposite of what the person who is judgmental seems to want.

What, then, is a more self-supportive choice if we find ourselves unhappy with a particular circumstance? The first step is to recognize that each of us, as creators of our lives, has brought the circumstance to us purposefully. And the purpose is always the same—to arouse feelings that we have repressed. All of our feelings want their freedom, and our inner knowing supports us, always, in freeing them.

Where we confuse ourselves and slow the process is in our attempts to make sense of circumstances. But the purpose of circumstances is not to make sense. Trying to understand them is always futile, particularly in the case of the more bizarre circumstances we create to arouse deeply repressed feelings.

So rather than trying to figure out a circumstance, it is helpful to recognize that anything that has the capacity to make us uncomfortable is something that we have vested with power. The existence and degree of importance of the circumstance is solely and exclusively our own creation.

The last step is to reclaim the power that we have vested outside of ourselves. The way we reclaim this power is through the Feeling Exercise. When we finally bring the energy that we have placed outside of ourselves back in, we learn that we are all-powerful and that the belief that anything outside of us has any impact on us is an illusion.

The only substance in the Universe is essence, which is all that we are. The rest is illusion. None of us wishes to change essence, we only wish to change illusion—and that is the biggest illusion of all.

46

———

DESIRE AND JOYFULNESS

Underneath our beliefs—the way we interpret everything that goes on in our lives—is pure consciousness, our essence. The feeling quality that accompanies our essence is joyfulness, which is our natural state.

Why do we have such a difficult time accepting this truth? Or put another way, why do we so vigorously resist being in our natural state of joyfulness?

One of the main reasons stems from our misperception that our physical bodies are real and that our essence is unreal. We each have been carefully taught, from our earliest days, that we *are* our physical bodies. Furthermore, this belief, constantly reinforced by all aspects of society, tells us that only the physical world is real and that if we can't see or touch something or measure it in some definable way, then the thing doesn't exist.

An extension of this belief is the perception that we improve the quality of our lives by having things—cars, houses, money in the bank, relationships and chocolate fudge sundaes. What is not yet clear to us is how our desire for these things corresponds with our desire for joyfulness.

Wanting things and having things is a neutral condition. What determines the impact of the desire is the accompanying state of consciousness. When our perception is that having something will make us feel better or improve the quality of our lives, we are reinforcing the belief that we are just physical bodies.

When we are in a state of joyfulness, and that state of being attracts to us something in the physical, we are merely demonstrating the truth that abundance is our natural state. Abundance is a fun partner and companion to joyfulness.

Stated another way, when we see the physical as cause, we are simply mislabeling effect. When we feel joyfulness—the feeling state of our essence—as cause, we are feeling who we really are. In our natural state of joyfulness, we are in the perfect place to attract abundance in any of its myriad forms, including physical things.

As we become comfortable residing in our natural state of joyfulness, we notice that we can have a full experience of something that has a physical reality merely by aligning with it in consciousness. Our essence is just a vibration, albeit a high vibration. Everything that appears in the physical is also a vibration, albeit a lower vibration. Aligning the two is simple when we are vibrating at the level of our essence.

When our consciousness is vibrating at the level of physicality, we are denying ourselves the feeling of joyfulness, which is a higher vibration. We also relegate "having" things to a feeling quality that is heavy and devoid of the fun and lightness of joyfulness. This is evident when the feeling of satisfaction that accompanies the receipt of some "thing" dissipates and is replaced by the perceived need to have some other thing.

We have negated our essence most of our lives. Why, then, should we suddenly accept its existence? Furthermore, how do we release the multitude of beliefs that have become our guidelines for living and that unequivocally and totally deny the existence of our essence?

The answer is found by acknowledging the motivation or force within you that led you to read this book. Our essence is not only real, it is and always will be our true power. And no matter how hard we may try to deny the existence or minimize the power of our essence, our essence remains who we truly are.

How, then, do we reach the joyfulness that is our true state of being? Simply by surrendering all of our beliefs, which are just fictitious overlays that have no more reality or substance than a fog. Remember that no matter how dense a fog, the sun is always shining. And we can always choose to move through the fog to the warmth and brightness of the sunshine.

So the real questions become: How important is it to be who we really are? And is this what we truly want? It is for each of us to answer these questions, and the answers will be yes only when we love ourselves enough to allow joyfulness, our natural state, to arise within us.

47

THOSE WARM,
FUZZY FEELINGS

O nce we accept ourselves as feeling beings, we are ready to learn to distinguish between feelings that flow from our essence and feelings that are superficial. The latter are ones that we create when we avoid connecting with the intense energies that we have buried deep within—our real feelings.

Having been taught that our real feelings can mislead us or make us vulnerable, we have learned to push them away and live apart from them. This repression of our feelings has not only caused us great pain, it has left us with the perception that we are powerless and at the effect of many forces beyond our control.

At the same time we learned to accept that our feelings are our weakness, we also were taught that our power lies in our intellects. The result of our acceptance of these misperceptions is that we have been battered by all kinds of events and circumstances, and each one has reinforced our belief in our powerlessness.

Since we are feeling beings, we substituted superficial feelings for the feelings deep within that we pushed away. These superficial feelings are ones that are connected to beliefs. And the belief that has become a sort of cornerstone of all others is the belief that love is divisible.

We have been taught that we can love some people and not others. In support of this belief, we create warm, fuzzy feelings when our perception is that we feel love for one particular person. We also create feelings of discomfort when we bring into consciousness someone we do not like.

In truth, love is indivisible. We are all One. There is no reality in the belief in separation. Therefore, a real feeling is one that flows out of our Oneness. We can feel such a feeling only when we release our attachment to the belief that we are separate.

Feeling our Oneness at a deep level connects us with our inner peace, our joyfulness and our true power. Those of us who have directly experienced this connection to our Oneness know the difference between our real feelings and superficial ones. We also know that both warm, fuzzy feelings and discomfort are signals to open our hearts and bring the energy in everything that seems separate from us back into our hearts.

Our hearts know our truth. Our hearts feel our Oneness, our joy and our power. When we are deeply in our hearts, we do not allow the illusion of warm, fuzzy feelings to take precedence over the real feelings that lie within.

48

———■———

HOW WOULD
YOU LIKE TO FEEL?

When you know that you are a feeling being, when you have opened your heart and felt deep love for yourself, you are ready for the advanced phase of the Feeling Exercise. The first three steps are the same. These are immediately followed by:

4. How would you like to feel? Feel the most wonderful feeling you are ready to feel.
5. Feel love for this feeling. Feel love for the energy, the power, in the feeling.
6. Feel love for yourself feeling this feeling. Feel love for yourself feeling the power in the feeling.

Your willingness to add these steps to the Feeling Exercise is a gift you give to yourself. It is a perfect way to expand your love for yourself.

As our love for ourselves expands, the importance of our physical world diminishes. The power that we vested in the physical is reclaimed, and we know and feel that we are the power in the Universe.

Feeling inner peace accompanied by joyfulness consistently, and feeling the fullness of our power in each present moment, is a choice. Do you love yourself enough to choose feeling wonderful in each present moment? Is this what "You Can Have It All" means to you?

49

COMMITMENT TO MASTERY

Mastery of the real game of life calls for 100 percent intention and commitment. As strange as it may sound, everyone is totally committed to whatever is going on in her life. This applies equally to a homeless person who seems to be wandering aimlessly through life as well as to an executive who has a plan for each waking moment of his life (and with subliminal tapes, for even non-waking moments).

In order to discover what we are committed to, we need only look at what is going on in our lives. Whatever circumstances are before us are ones our essence has brought to us in support of what we have intended to accomplish in this lifetime.

We can align with this process by connecting with our life purpose at a deep feeling level and in a state of conscious awareness. Making this connection requires the willingness to feel, in our open hearts, all the feelings that are attached to beliefs that undermine our acceptance of who we really are.

The alternative, chosen by many, is to back away from these feelings, which are often intense. The result is a sense that there are powerful forces outside of us that are in control of our lives.

For those of us who say to ourselves that we would really like to feel the fullness of our true feelings and reclaim the power in them, but who still feel only the warm, fuzzy feelings or the discomfort, it is important to recognize that we are committed to the latter. In order to feel our true feelings, then, we have to consciously make the commitment.

To whom do we make this commitment? Most of us were taught that commitments are made to others. The truth is that we can commit only to ourselves. Others are just reflections of the state of our own consciousness. We are always looking at and feeling aspects of ourselves.

We are ready to commit to feeling our real feelings—our inner peace, joyfulness and power—only when we love ourselves enough to give ourselves this magnificent gift. The path to feeling the feelings of our essence, our True Self, is a day-by-day, moment-by-moment commitment to feeling love for ourselves just the way we are.

Eventually this love for our Self grows to include all selves. And we know in every molecule of our infinite being that we are One.

Are you ready to commit to loving all of you until you feel the magnificent fullness of who you are? That is the price of mastery. That is what it takes to have it all.

50

BEYOND BELIEFS

B eliefs are not natural to us. And keeping our beliefs alive is
exhausting. In those moments when we are just too tired to
hold on to a belief, we gain a glimpse of life beyond beliefs. Also in
those moments, without realizing it, we surrender to our natural state
of being, our essence, and to the feeling quality that accompanies that
state, our joyfulness.

Our essence floats in an ocean of joy, surrounded by abundance
and unconditional love. The glimpses we allow ourselves of our
natural state are signals that we are ready to accept the gift that is
always being offered to us.

Mansions, Rolls-Royces and millions of dollars are never an
adequate substitute for the joy that fills our being when we open our
hearts to feel the depth of our love for ourselves. And the unconditional love we wish to feel from others is held at bay until we are
ready to first feel this deep and abiding love we have for ourselves.

Can you hear the sound of that ocean of joy beckoning? Can you feel the nurturing warmth of unconditional love moving in to embrace you? Can you sense the sigh of relief within as you surrender to ecstasy?

Enjoy!

A Summary of
Universal Principles

Universal Principles are the guidelines that govern our lives perfectly.

1. Energy

The basic component of the Universe, energy, occurs in either materialized or unmaterialized form. All that we see and feel is an expression of energy

Energy is synonymous with love. When we resist the flow of energy, or love, we experience discomfort. When we align with the energy flowing around and through us, we feel joyful and at peace.

2. Infinite Intelligence, or God

Within all energy is an Intelligence that is infinite, eternal and purposeful. This Infinite Intelligence, which we sometimes refer to as God, or simply love, is the source of all creative expression and the essential power in the Universe.

The way we view our Infinite Intelligence, or God, is precisely the way we experience life. When we perceive God as an unconditionally loving and supportive energy at all times and under all circumstances, we experience our world and everyone in it as totally safe, loving and generous.

3. Oneness

Since the essence of everything is pure loving energy, in the truest sense, *we are one*. When we feel our connection to our Oneness, we feel the power of who we really are.

Our Oneness, love, is indivisible, and thus it is not possible to love one thing or person more than another. Whenever we attempt to withhold love from anyone, we withhold love from everyone, including ourselves. The truth of this principle becomes clear to us as we allow our hearts to open and feel our interconnectedness.

4. PERFECTION

Our Oneness, God, is perfect and expresses this perfection in infinite ways. As human beings, we are created, and we function, perfectly just the way we are.

When someone or something appears to be less than perfect, we know that we have chosen to feel disconnected from our Oneness. We feel connected when our hearts are open. When our hearts are open wide, we see and feel the perfection of everything.

5. CAUSE AND EFFECT

Contrary to what we have been taught, we are not at the effect of the circumstances in our lives. We are the creators of these circumstances. And we create these circumstances with great purposefulness.

The creation occurs at two levels. At one level, cause is put into motion by our Infinite Intelligence. We create at this level when we are in a state of peacefulness and when we trust our Infinite Intelligence to guide and support us.

At another level, cause is set in motion by our thinking minds. What we believe creates our experiences.

6. FREE WILL

We each have the freedom to choose in each moment. We can choose for ourselves, but not for others. When we allow others to choose for us, we withdraw our trust in ourselves to make choices. Accepting the choice another makes for us is our choice.

When we consciously choose to let Infinite Intelligence guide us, our lives unfold in effortless and magnificent ways.

7. BELIEFS AND ILLUSIONS

Our beliefs—both conscious and unconscious—determine our experiences. We can recognize what we believe by noticing the experiences in which we find ourselves.

Our beliefs are illusions; they are not real. By quieting our minds and focusing our awareness on what is real—our Oneness—we move beyond our illusory beliefs and experience the inherent perfection of the Universe.

8. Intuition, Feelings and Power

Our Infinite Intelligence communicates to us through our intuition, which we access through our feelings. The more willing we are to feel our feelings, the more able we are to connect with the power that resides in them.

The true power in the Universe is a totally peaceful power. It is the power of love, fully, freely and joyfully felt.

9. Mutual Support

Our Universe functions as a mutual support system in which each and every thing in existence relates to and affects every other thing. Every person and circumstance in our lives is there to support us by reflecting back to us the present state of our consciousness.

Despite the prevalent belief that we are naturally competitive and adversarial, we always have the choice to create environments that are harmonious, nurturing and mutually supportive. Choosing to join with others who share a commitment to living in mutual support is both self-loving and empowering.

10. The Mirror Principle

Everything that we see and feel is a reflection of the state of our own consciousness. Every person we attract into our lives is showing us some aspect of who we are. Every feeling expressed by another mirrors a feeling deep within us.

This reflection is a gift, for it allows us to be aware of the beliefs we hold. We then have the choice to reclaim the power we have vested in our beliefs.

11. NONJUDGMENT AND FORGIVENESS

We have each been carefully taught to evaluate and judge virtually
everything we experience. However, there is no such thing as right or
wrong, good or bad. Everything that occurs is just another event. By
judging something, it becomes for us the way we judge it, and it stays that
way until we release the judgment.

Judging anyone or anything as being less than perfect blocks our
ability to respond to the essence of the person or thing and creates
discomfort within us that can only be relieved by opening our hearts,
first to the judgment and then to the person or thing we have judged.

Forgiveness is the willingness to open the energy locked up in our
judgments. Opening our hearts allows forgiveness to expand into
unconditional love.

12. PURPOSE

Everything and everyone in the Universe has a purpose for existing. As
we each become aware of our life's purpose, we increase our sense of
belonging and see the deeper meaning of our lives.

We become aware of our purpose by opening our hearts and feeling
our Oneness. When we allow the inspiration of our life's purpose to fill
our being, we find that our lives unfold in inspired, fulfilling ways.

13. COMFORT AND DISCOMFORT

Our human bodies are magnificent instruments that tell us at all times
just how aligned we are with the energy flowing around and through us.

Discomfort in our bodies is a signal that we are resisting the flow
of energy, or love. The greater the discomfort, the more we know we are
resisting giving and receiving love.

As soon as we notice discomfort, whether physical, mental or
emotional, we best support ourselves by focusing our awareness on our
feelings, feeling them fully, and then feeling love for them and for
ourselves. When we allow love to flow freely, our bodies reflect this
free flow of energy.

14.   ABUNDANCE AND GRATITUDE

Abundance is the natural state of the Universe. It is the free flow of energy, which is literally all around us, in infinite supply, and available to everyone who is open to receive it.

If we are experiencing less than total abundance in each and every aspect of our lives, we know we are resisting the natural flow of abundance. We open to abundance by feeling gratitude for all that we presently have.

15.   GIVING AND RECEIVING

Giving and receiving always occur in balance. It is as important to receive gratefully as it is to give voluntarily, generously, and with no expectations. Our willingness to keep the energy flowing in and out of our lives supports the energy in expanding.

The corollary to the principle of giving and receiving is that we give only to ourselves. Since we are all One, when we give to another, we are really giving to ourselves.

16.   NONATTACHMENT AND FREEDOM

Our perceived need to hold on to anything or anyone demonstrates our belief in shortage. Holding on to anything—people or possessions—blocks the flow of energy around our experience with the person or object and reduces the joy of the experience. It also inhibits new people and new things from coming into our lives.

As we open our hearts and expand our trust in the natural abundance of the Universe, we give ourselves and everyone else the gift of freedom.

17.   WHAT WE FOCUS ON EXPANDS

We are free to focus our attention wherever we choose. We can focus on what we perceive to be problems, or we can remind ourselves that every circumstance is an opportunity to reclaim the power we have vested in our beliefs.

When we focus on our pure feelings, unencumbered by beliefs, what expands within and around us is peace, joy and abundance.

18. Expressing Who We Really Are

Each of us has one or more talents we love to express. When we are fully and freely expressing who we really are, we feel joyful and supported.

What determines how successful we will be at expressing our talents is how much love we feel for ourselves. The more love we feel for ourselves, the more we allow the creative energy of the Universe to flow through us. Freely expressing who we are leads us to feel our perfection, so that our perfection expands.

19. Means and Ends

Means and ends are the same. The action and outcome are one.

To achieve peace, we feel and express our inner peacefulness. To enjoy a life that works perfectly, we see and feel the perfection of everything and everyone, including ourselves. To experience the natural abundance of the Universe, we feel and express gratitude for the abundance all around us.

20. Harmony in Relationships

Every relationship in our lives reflects our relationship with ourselves. Every person we attract is there to support us in opening our hearts and reclaiming our power.

When we truly love ourselves and feel the power and perfection that we are, we attract loving, harmonious relationships with others.

21. The Universe Handles the Details

Taking care of the details of our lives is generally considered a rational-mind activity. However, when our rational minds are active, we shut out our Infinite Intelligence, which has the capacity to handle the details in ways that are vastly more supportive of us and everyone else.

As we learn to relinquish our rational thinking and surrender to our intuition—our connection to Infinite Intelligence—we discover how easily, effortlessly and spontaneously events unfold for us.

8

Arnold Patent
Workshops and Workshop Tapes

Over the past fifteen years, Arnold Patent has led hundreds of workshops and seminars across the United States and in Canada, England and Holland. These workshops offer participants the opportunity to learn about Universal Principles and the mutual support model in a relaxed, focused and highly enjoyable way.

Out of the workshop experience, participants are inspired to form support groups in their local areas, so that they can continue to practice the principles in a loving, supportive environment. There are now in existence no-cost mutual support groups throughout the United States and in Canada, Central America, Western Europe, the Middle East and Australia.

The Mutual Support Group Handbook contains everything you need to facilitate a mutual support group meeting. Developed over a decade, the clearly annotated handbook includes: guidelines for support group meetings, an easy-to-follow format, the Invocation and Power of Peace Meditation, explanations for defining the group purpose as well as individual purposes, and a variety of simple yet profound exercises that can help support and empower participants. The handbook also includes a summary of Universal Principles.

For information about sponsoring or attending an Arnold Patent workshop, to order *The Mutual Support Group Handbook* or for assistance in joining or forming a mutual support group in your area, call:
MUTUAL SUPPORT NETWORK 1-800-828-4308